In this book, *Mindset–Reset,* Charles Westmoreland shows that the driving force behind anyone's success is their mindset. Whether you think you can or think you can't, you are right. The choice is yours. Open your mind as you open this book to discover the path to your destiny.

—Dr. Christopher Bowen

If you have spent years in misery trying to figure out the reason you keep going around in circles, *Mindset–Reset* is a wonderful guide to self-mastery. This will be a catalyst for your newfound freedom. Heal your mind, and you will heal your body.

—Joseph C. Verdun, MD

Do you continue in the same unwanted cycles year after year, shifting back and forth from one relationship to another? *Mindset–Reset* is an outstanding book that will shed impeccable light and set you on a revised journey toward a brighter future.

—Mayor Anthony S. Ford
City of Stockbridge, Georgia

It has been a joy and a pleasure to mentor Charles Westmoreland in the area of bringing theology and science together. His open heart and mind have accelerated his learning. But the most exciting thing to me is how he and his family have immediately implemented their gained knowledge and understanding. Charles didn't stop there. He has been doing a monthly meeting titled

"Inspire" to pass his understanding on to others. These meetings have been met with enthusiasm and requests for additional meetings. This is because the attendees are learning, implementing the information, and experiencing happier and more fulfilled lives. His meetings are electrified with info, music, and digital photos. I admire his desire and humble heart to help others on their earthly journey. Therefore, *Mindset–Reset* has evolved with others to follow.

—Dr. Carolyn Driver

MINDSET

CHANGE
YOUR
THINKING

TRANSFORM
YOUR
REALITY

RESET

CHARLES WESTMORELAND

DREAM RELEASER
PUBLISHING

Scripture quotations marked KJV are taken from the King James Version of the Bible. Public domain. | Scripture quotations marked NIV are taken from the Holy Bible, New International Version®, NIV®. Copyright © 1973, 1978, 1984, 2011 by Biblica, Inc.™ Used by permission of Zondervan. All rights reserved worldwide. www.zondervan.com. The "NIV" and "New International Version" are trademarks registered in the United States Patent and Trademark Office by Biblica, Inc.™ | Scripture quotations marked NKJV are taken from the New King James Version®. Copyright © 1982 by Thomas Nelson. Used by permission. All rights reserved. | Scripture quotations marked ESV are from The ESV® Bible (The Holy Bible, English Standard Version®), copyright © 2001 by Crossway, a publishing ministry of Good News Publishers. Used by permission. All rights reserved.

For foreign and subsidiary rights, contact the author.

Cover design by: Sara Young

Cover Photo by: Andrew van Tilborgh

ISBN: _978-1-959095-02-6   1 2 3 4 5 6 7 8 9 10

Printed in the United States of America

I dedicate this book to men and women all over the world who carry around the weight and the burden of guilt and shame because of the many self-sabotaging ideas that have taken root within their subconscious minds. I pray that you will find the strength, comfort, and hope that you so desperately desire within these pages and through the process of doing the work of inner healing. May you be released from the clutching grasp of your sleeping giant. I further dedicate this book to the many people who have pushed and supported me along the way. You all have been such a vital part of my journey, and I am eternally grateful—for my friends, professors, assistants, and family who have believed in and invested in me!

CONTENTS

FOREWORD

"A mind is a terrible thing to waste." We've all heard that in a variety of contexts, and no one in their right mind—pun intended—would disagree with that. However, minds are wasted by the millions daily, primarily because of faulty mindsets. This book, *Mindset-Reset*, by Pastor Charles Westmoreland explores just that.

We are all born with inherent mental capacities and good mental software that gets hacked by those usually closest to us. Our environment and those around us influence us in greater measure than we realize. For example, why does a baby speak the language of his or her parent? Because parents write their children's software. The same baby born in Japan would speak Japanese as would the same baby—if born in France—speak French. A baby is programmed to speak every language of the world but speaks the language of their environment. That is a simple illustration of a totally innocuous and natural influence of family and friends.

Unfortunately, one's expectations and ways of thinking, understanding, responding, learning, dreaming, etc., end up on a continuum of healthy to toxic. I see patterns of behavior in my own life that were created as a young child—for better or worse. In many, not all cases, I've been able to move the needle toward health, and I'm working on the others. In my book *New Thinking–New Future*, I postulate that to have a new future, we need new thinking. As you read this book—based on the Bible and credible research—try your best to not let old thinking censor and preempt a *Mindset–Reset*.

—Sam Chand

ACKNOWLEDGMENTS

To my amazing wife of thirty-five years, Deloris—you have never failed to show your unwavering support for my every endeavor. I'm so glad I get the opportunity to do life with you. I'm looking forward to many more years of love, life, and happiness together. I love you.

To my son, Darius—you continue to be one of the greatest joys of my life. Watching you grow up and become the man that you are, taking on the world and creating your world, and building a platform for other young men to share their giftings gives me extreme joy. I'm so proud to call you son.

To my sister, Jackie Muscovalley—you have always been one of my strongest supporters. For as long as I can remember, you've been there, loving and pushing me even with this project. Thanks!

Dr. Carolyn Driver, thank you for the countless hours of impartation, guidance, and wisdom that you have so unselfishly given to me over the years and especially with this project. You are such a priceless gift to my life and to the world.

To my Restoration/Inspire community, this journey with you has been amazing. Your love, support, and encouragement have been a source of fuel in a most amazing way. Seeing the transformation that's taking place in the lives of so many of you is so rewarding. Thank you for allowing me the opportunity to serve you in this capacity! We have walked the path of great victory for the past ten years together, and I look forward to what is yet to come for us as we continue to walk and work together.

To my heavenly Father, I owe You everything. You are indeed my all and all. Thank You doesn't even begin to scratch the surface as it relates to my level of gratitude for what You have been for me and the things You have done. Thank You for this new place in You, a place of maturation that I never even knew was possible. Thank You for Your love that comforts, Your peace that guides, and Your grace that sustains. My heart's desire is to serve You and to honor You—with every fiber of my being—for the duration of my days.

INTRODUCTION

Reset: to set, adjust, or fix in
a new or different way[1]

And, of course, my focus is a different way.

As I look at the state of the world, I see so many people being
affected by the hidden wounds lying deep within their souls. We
go through life in constant conflict with others, unable to connect, many times with the ones dearest to us. We live in captive
isolation, all because we don't have the wherewithal to conquer
holes in our souls—the places that have been broken and left
empty, such as:

---

1 "Reset Definition & Meaning," *Dictionary.com*, https://www.dictionary.com/browse/reset.

1) **Unmet needs that have persisted in our lives for years.**

We as human beings are wired to need comfort and attention just as much as we need food and oxygen. Therefore, if we grew up in an environment where we could not always count on our caregivers to be there when we needed them, we likely view these absences as life-threatening and have developed an emotional deficiency as a result of these unmet needs.

2) **Unhealed hurts that have intensified.**

When you have been traumatized in life, it lives deep inside of you. You could even say it settles in your bones. The memories, even if pushed away and not conscious, are etched into you and evident by your symptoms, relationship struggles, and poor self-esteem.

3) **Unresolved issues that create deep pain.**

Unresolved feelings such as anger and hostility can have an adverse effect on your overall health and state of being. They can directly impact your heart health.

In the process of reading *Mindset–Reset*, you will find phrases and themes that have been intentionally repeated. Studies have shown that you must hear something sixteen times before you own it. Also, you will find affirmations that should be repeated *out loud*. This is to aid in memory retention.

I have written this book with sincere hopes that you will make a decision today—to take charge of your thoughts . . . which will lead to different emotions . . . which, in return, will RESET your mind. You are literally one decision away from a different life and a different you. Say no to the old habits that keep yielding unfruitful results and yes to a new outlook. I pray that as you are reading, you make a decision to refuse to settle for less than God's best when it comes to the state of your emotions and the quality of your life.

CHAPTER 1

OF TWO MINDS

F or years, I've pondered what the topic would be for this book. I often thought of writing about relationships because I know and have experienced the value of having healthy, fruitful relationships. I know the difference they can make and the impact they can have on your life and your destiny.

I thought of writing about health and fitness because it has become one of my greatest passions as I've seen so many people around me and in my family suffer from sickness and disease all because of a lack of discipline in terms of what they eat. This has proven to be a source of fuel that has given me the extra determination not to travel the same path but to live my life in a way that I could remain fruitful even into my senior years of life. My mother, seeing that I had made this a mantra for my life, said to me before she passed away, "I like the way you take that exercise every day. When you get to my age, you won't have all these ailments in your body."

I often thought of writing about finances because my perspective on money has certainly taken on a different outlook. Growing up and listening to so many different opinions about money and finances, I was not able to clearly deduce what I felt was the correct perspective on finances. Therefore, I was unable to experience the financial freedom and bliss that I was designed to walk in. However, God allowed me—for seven years—to sit under the tutelage of a dear friend and mentor to clear my viewpoint on finances and money. For that, I am eternally grateful! This encounter changed my financial mindset and status greatly.

I thought of writing about my faith as it is the principal foundation upon which my life and success are built. But after much deliberation of mind and heart, I settled on a place that I believe is an area that touches and affects all of these areas. And that is the mind. You see, it is with the mind that we are able to embrace all of the beauty of life. Therefore, what I would like for us to open up and explore in this book is that the mind can either work for us or against us, and we are in complete control of how that plays out.

MOST PEOPLE LIVE THEIR LIVES OBLIVIOUS TO THE FACT THAT THEY WILL EITHER BE IN CONTROL OF THEIR MIND OR BE CONTROLLED BY IT.

Most people live their lives oblivious to the fact that they will either be in control of their mind or be controlled by it. From the beginning, we were created and given free will. How is it then that many people live in complete bondage, driven and controlled by the emotions that are created by their thoughts and thoughts that are created by circumstances? One of the purposes of this book is to free you from the debilitating cycle that is lodged deep within your subconscious mind that continuously shows up in a self-sabotaging way to cripple you and ultimately take your life.

As a fully committed Christian, lead pastor, and follower of Jesus Christ, I believe that the Bible is the infallible truth. I also believe that it is imperative, as stated by the apostle Paul, that we should forever be of the persuasion that renewing our minds is an everyday process. He tells us this in Romans 12:2 (KJV): "And be not conformed to this world: but be ye transformed by the renewing of your mind." It is my desire to show you—with simplicity—that it is of the utmost importance that we intentionally take control of our thoughts. Only when we do this will we take control of our emotions, and that outcome will lead us to living a more victorious life.

Dr. Bruce Lipton, in his article, "THINK Beyond Your Genes," states that one's consciousness is the creative mind, and the subconsciousness is the programmed mind—the habit mind.[2] In his study, he discusses the nature of how our lives have been programmed and how these programs control our lives, our vitality, and our behavior. Recognize this. If you buy a new computer and turn it on, the built-in operating system prepares it to work. However, if there are no programs on that computer, then the computer can't really do anything. Let's relate this to a child. Dr. Lipton says that when the brain develops, it's got an operating system, but there are no programs on it. So nature created the first

---

2 Bruce H. Lipton, PhD, "Think Beyond Your Genes," *BruceLipton*, 16 Dec. 2021, https://www.brucelipton.com/think-beyond-your-genes-december-2021/.

seven years of our lives to download behavior by observing our parents, siblings, and our community.[3] This way, a child learns all the behavioral characteristics necessary to be a functional member of a family and community.

However, since we are downloading other programs by watching other people, what happens if we download programs that are not very positive? They are actually very negative programs that have an adverse effect on our health. Contemplating the direction I wanted to go with this book, Dr. Lipton's concept really proved to be an amazing way to share my thought processes. Using the metaphor of a computer and how it is constructed brings a great level of focus to the concept that I am trying to relay. These studies certainly correspond with my heart and my thought processes.

We often wonder why people do the things that they do, why they say the things that they say, and why certain patterns that we see in families seem to be continuously perpetuated from generation to generation. I wholeheartedly believe that Dr. Lipton's study— along with many others—brings validation to the fact that people are a product of their environment. His study further reveals that young children function in a state of hypnosis characteristic of a brain frequency called *theta*, which is just below consciousness.[4] When consciousness kicks in, at around age seven, it has use of programs to create the behavior patterns in their relationships with their family and community.

3 Bruce Lipton, PhD, "Reprogram Your Subconscious Mind with These 3 Powerful Steps," *Fearless Soul*, 8 July 2019, https://iamfearlesssoul.com/reprogram-your-subconscious-mind-with-these-3-powerful-steps-bruce-lipton/.
4 Bruce H. Lipton, PhD, "Think Beyond Your Genes."

I certainly concur with this finding from his study. Two years ago, I was blessed with my first granddaughter, Zoe. The joy and fulfillment that she brings to my life in all that she encounters are amazing. Embracing this concept of *theta* being a period of downloads is relevant and prevalent in my interaction with little Zoe. Coming home from the hospital, she had to be taught a sleep schedule (download). She had to be taught how to go from the bottle to baby food to regular food (download). She has progressed from communicating by crying to the use of words (download) and from dependence to independence.

We allow her, at her request, to do things like buckling her own seatbelt and feeding herself. These are things that build her confidence and independence. In the process, we celebrate her when she successfully accomplishes her task; this brings a form of positive affirmation. What we are finding is that this is teaching her to celebrate her own accomplishments. For instance, she will complete a task and yell out, "Yay, Zoe, I did it!" (download). Recently my son and I took her to the pool. When we started, she was in a floaty that completely supported her. It was used to get her comfortable with the water. From there, we moved to a type of floaty that would give her more mobility and control. Eventually, she was able to balance herself and did not want or need the support of her father (download).

**I SAID TO HER, "ZOE, WHO'S THE SWEETIE BABY?"
THEN I WOULD SAY TO HER, "SAY, 'ME!'"**

Noticing that Zoe had a major ability to learn quickly, I began to give her tests.

I said to her, "Zoe, who's the sweetie baby?" Then I would say to her, "Say, 'Me!'"

She would smile and, with excitement, say, "Me!"

After this one setting, it became a term of endearment between Zoe and me. Incidentally, it was something that my mother did with Zoe's father.

One day, I was standing in my closet, Zoe came into the closet, and she saw me standing there thinking, pondering, *What am I going to select from my closet?* Zoe looked at me and said, "Pop-Pop, what you think?"

I looked at Zoe and said, "I think I love you."

Zoe smiled at me, and from that moment on, she constantly has asked me randomly, "Pop-Pop, what you think?" She understands that my response will be, "I love you!" So this has become a form of affirmation between the two of us (download).

I hope that these simple illustrations have given you a visual and contextual analogy of how the *theta* theory hugely impacts us— whether positively or negatively—for years to come. Understand that these thoughts were embedded within our subconscious mind for seven years as programs that are controlling our actions today.

It is imperative that we examine and identify the patterns that we are exemplifying and make sure they are not negative or having adverse effects on our health.

Scientists have discovered that 70 percent of those programs that we download from others are negative, disempowering, and even self-sabotaging.[5] You might ask, "Where are these programs?" Great question! They're in the subconscious mind. The other mind, the conscious mind that kicks in at age seven, is connected to your personal identity and spirituality. The difference between the two is profound. According to Dr. Lipton, the conscious mind is a creative mind, and if you're running from the conscious mind, then you're creating your life from wishes, desires, and aspirations.[6] Dr. Lipton goes on to say, however, that "if your life is under the control of the subconscious mind, it's just going to play back the programs that you downloaded from other people. Since other people didn't plan your wishes and your desires, the download you get may not even allow you to get"[7] the life that you really wish for.

For example, Johnny, after coming into the knowledge of his conscious mind, decides that he wants to build his life and become a great attorney. Johnny feels that he has the ability to argue his case with any issue and win. However, even though Johnny believes this, there are programs that have been downloaded and

5 Robin Galante, "4 Things to Remember the next Time You're Spiraling," *Headspace*, https://www.headspace.com/articles/4-things-remember-next-time-youre-spiraling.
6 Bruce H. Lipton, PhD, "Do You Understand Your Mind?" *BruceLipton*, 10 July 2014, https://www.brucelipton.com/do-you-understand-your-mind/.
7 Bruce Lipton, PhD, "Reprogram Your Subconscious Mind with These 3 Powerful Steps," *Fearless Soul*, 8 July 2019, https://iamfearlesssoul.com/reprogram-your-subconscious-mind-with-these-3-powerful-steps-bruce-lipton/.

embedded for years in his subconscious mind that don't support it. If Johnny does not do the work of deleting those programs and resetting with a new mindset, those defeating, self-sabotaging thoughts and habits will continuously fight against his thoughts of a better life.

We all struggle with this, and one of the reasons we struggle is that we have not embraced the concept that there is something deep within us that is keeping us from being the best expression of ourselves. It is my desire that as you read this book, it will shed light on the deep, dark places where these things tend to hide and breed, leading you to understand that any darkness brought to the light loses its power over you. What is it that has kept you from exploring the dream? What is it that has kept you from starting the business, running a marathon, or connecting with the person that you feel is your life partner? This is the time—this is the season—for you to confront your unmet needs, unhealed hurts, and unresolved issues. Only then will you be free from the agony of your subconscious mind.

THIS IS THE TIME—THIS IS THE SEASON—FOR YOU TO CONFRONT YOUR UNMET NEEDS, UNHEALED HURTS, AND UNRESOLVED ISSUES. ONLY THEN WILL YOU BE FREE FROM THE AGONY OF YOUR SUBCONSCIOUS MIND.

WHAT IF...

What would you say if I told you that you were on the verge of being the best expression of you that has ever walked the face of the earth?

_____

_____

What if I told you that the poverty you are experiencing—or have experienced—is just a vehicle that has been used to prepare you to release and unveil all of the greatness that lives inside your soul?

_____

_____

What if I told you that the imperfections you behold when you look at your life are the sum total of the unique qualities that have made you in the likeness and the image of who He created you to be?

_____

_____

What if I told you that even though you may have experienced great love, peace, joy, and overwhelming success in your life that the best days of your life are in front of you?

_____

_____

CHAPTER 2

GOOD VIBRATIONS

Your mind possesses two distinctive characteristics whose functions are essentially unalike. Joseph Murphy wrote, "Each is endowed with separate and distinct attributes and powers. The nomenclature generally used to distinguish the two"[8] is as follows:

» **conscious**—aware of and responding to one's surroundings, awake.[9]

» **subconscious**—the part of the mind of which one is not fully aware but which influences one's actions and emotions.[10]

It is your responsibility to stand guard, monitoring what goes into your conscious mind. Because the conscious mind is the gateway to the subconscious mind, anything that you allow to enter your conscious mind goes into your subconscious mind, and your subconscious mind begins to work on bringing it to life or to manifestation.

---

8 "The Power of Your Subconscious Mind—Joseph Murphy, Chapter 1—The Treasure House Within You—Part 1," *The Linguist Institute*, https://www.lingq.com/en/learn-english-online/courses/233550/chapter-1-the-treasure-house-within-yo-743771/.
9 "Conscious English Definition and Meaning," *Lexico Dictionaries | English*, Lexico Dictionaries, https://www.lexico.com/en/definition/conscious.
10 "Subconscious English Definition and Meaning," *Lexico Dictionaries | English*, Lexico Dictionaries, https://www.lexico.com/en/definition/subconscious.

ANYTHING THAT YOU ALLOW TO ENTER YOUR CONSCIOUS MIND GOES INTO YOUR SUBCONSCIOUS MIND, AND YOUR SUBCONSCIOUS MIND BEGINS TO WORK ON BRINGING IT TO LIFE OR TO MANIFESTATION.

Through your conscious mind, you take in thoughts. Every seventeen seconds, you get a thought to add to your other thoughts which means you get four supporting thoughts in a minute. If you do the math, every hour, you get a total of 240 supporting thoughts. After eight hours, you have 1,920 thoughts. These can be positive or negative. When they become negative, you have to take control and replace the negative with positive thoughts. Never underestimate the power of your subconscious mind! It is a powerful thing, and it is always at work.

There have been numerous occasions when a loved one, friend, or acquaintance has been in the hospital, not able to speak, and/ or the doctor states they are unconscious. In many instances, the patient has been told, "If you hear me, squeeze my hand, or wiggle your toe." Because the subconscious mind is always at work, the response is received from the patient. This is why your conscious and subconscious minds must be congruent. They must be saying the same thing, but there is always a constant battle between the conscious and subconscious minds. You have the power to control this battle, and if you don't embrace self-mastery, you will always live a life of instability.

The Bible puts it this way in James 1:6-8 (KJV):

> *But let him ask in faith, nothing wavering. For he that wavereth is like a wave of the sea driven with the wind and tossed. For let not that man think that he shall receive any thing of the Lord. A double minded man is unstable in all his ways.*

If your words, emotions, and visualizations are incongruent, you are double-minded, and chances are, when you ask in prayer for something specific, you are going to hit the delete button by speaking negatively, visualizing a negative outcome, or harboring negative supporting thoughts. Therefore, you'll be deleting your dreams, desires, and written strategies for life. To conquer this, you must have a daily practice of immersion in the practice of self-mastery.

I sincerely hope that by the time you have reached the last chapter of this book, your mindset will have been renewed, you will be on a journey to a brand new you, and your heart you will be able to say, "I want everything that life has to offer me!" Will you repeat the following affirmation out loud? "I'm a good person, and good things are supposed to happen to me. I deserve a good life, and I'm not wrong for thinking that way."

Getting in touch with and learning to control the subconscious you is what we call self-mastery. This will be the greatest level of success that you could ever achieve in your life. It will be paramount to anything else that you have ever done or could ever do.

My awakening this morning was to the beat of a different drum. I could hear in the distance the sound of the gentle waves lapping at the sands of the shore. That sound brought about a sense of peace and serenity. I got up out of the bed and walked out onto the balcony which overlooked the ocean. I could clearly see and embrace the emerging sun with its rays glistening down upon the ocean. What an amazing sight! This brought to mind so many different thoughts. The first thought was, *What a magnificent God we serve—He is able to tell the water to stop at the banks of the shore.*

Then, the realization hit me that He was the same God who created me and gave me dominion over all of the things that I was casting my eyes upon. This brought a great sense of purpose and value to me, knowing that He thinks so much of us that He gave us rulership over all that He created. That is enough to inspire us to get up and take control of our lives.

According to BBC Bitesize:

> *In Genesis, the term dominion means to rule over nature. This is the idea that humans are in charge of the world on behalf of God. Some Christians, who have a literal interpretation of the Bible, believe that this gives humans the right to use the world's natural resources for their own benefit.*[11]

---

11 "Dominion—The World—GCSE Religious Studies Revision," *BBC News*, https://www.bbc.co.uk/bitesize/guides/zqphw6f/revision/5.

Dominion touches every part of our being. And despite our fallen state, God has not removed the charge to rule over the earth from humanity. Therefore, we must consider how to use the authority God has given us to bring Him glory and take control of our world. Please understand that the greatest level of dominion we could ever have is dominion over ourselves. If we can conquer us, we will be fully equipped to conquer the world. Therefore, the premise of this book is to teach you how to have dominion over your thoughts which will, in turn, give you dominion over your world.

HAVING DOMINION OVER YOUR THOUGHTS WILL GIVE YOU DOMINION OVER YOUR WORLD.

Thoughts are real and have a vibrational frequency. More positive thoughts have a higher vibrational frequency, and sad thoughts have a low vibrational frequency.[12] Additionally, like frequency attracts like frequency.[13] So we continue to attract either positive or negative things.

12 Christina Lopez, "The Science Behind Good Vibrations," *BALANCE*, 31 Jan. 2020, https://balance.media/good-vibrations/#:~:text=Positive%20vibrations%20are%20high%2Dfrequency,we%20feel%20resistance%20within%20ourselves.
13 Paul Thomas, "The Law of Vibration Explained: How to Make It Work Wonders for You," *Self Help for Life*, Paul Thomas Https://Selfhelpforlife.com/Wp-Content/Uploads/2017/08/Self-Help-Logo-White-BG-Blue-095da1-.Png, 11 Aug. 2021, https://selfhelpforlife.com/law-of-vibration-explained/.

We must also embrace the fact that we are not our thoughts. Just because you have a thought doesn't mean that you are the thought. Thoughts can come from many different places: God, Satan, education, erroneous theology, culture, unhealed hurts, unmet needs, unresolved issues, etc. The conscious mind is supposed to be your gatekeeper and stop thoughts that produce low vibrational energy. It is our job to replace them with thoughts that produce higher vibrational energy, and by doing that, we will attract additional higher energy resulting in more positive thoughts. God doesn't judge you for the thoughts that you have because of their many different sources. What matters the most is what you do with the thought when it comes. The conscious mind either embraces it or rejects it and replaces it with a better thought.

For instance, let me share with you a personal story. One brisk fall morning, I woke up and sat on the side of the bed with great anticipation for a powerful day. My phone rang, and I answered the call. The person on the other end began to voice their concerns about the way I had handled a situation. This proceeded for about six minutes nonstop. I interrupted with hopes of bringing clarity to my actions—only to be interrupted. Once again, they proceeded to question my integrity. I could clearly see that my explanations were not being heard, so I brought the conversation to a close, furious.

I continued my day. I got dressed, got in the car, and asked myself a question: *Is this the day you anticipated when you sat on the side of the bed?* The answer was no, so I immediately went to work to shift my energy. I said to myself, *Charles, you are a good man.*

You desire to provoke the good in all of the people in your circle, and good things are supposed to come back to you. I repeated this several times, and I could feel the energy in the car shifting to a higher vibrational frequency. Immediately, I began to recognize what was happening. I went a step further, and I played my favorite motivational song. The atmosphere shifted even higher. I continued this pattern for forty-five minutes, and by the time I arrived at my destination for my first meeting, I was ready to conquer the world. That was solely because I made a decision to take charge of my world. My meeting was a great success, I formed a new partnership that would take my business to a higher level, and the rest of my day was absolutely phenomenal. All because I took control of my thoughts, my emotions, and my will, the end result was a phenomenal day.

What if I told you that this was God's will for you every day, and if you practice the principles given in this book, you can live this life every day of your life?

THOUGHTS ARE WHAT PRODUCE YOUR EMOTIONAL STATE, AND YOU CAN CHANGE YOUR EMOTIONAL STATE IN A SECOND BY CHANGING YOUR THOUGHTS.

Thoughts are what produce your emotional state, and you can change your emotional state in a second by changing your thoughts. Thoughts produce emotions, and emotions produce a chemical called neuropeptide. This was discovered by Dr. Candace Pert in her book *Molecules of Emotion*.[14] The data in her study showed that good thoughts produce good neuropeptides. Negative thoughts produce toxic neuropeptides. Whatever chemical neuropeptides you're producing circulate through your body and go to every cell and every cell's receptor. Some cells have hundreds of receptors, and that's why thoughts could actually be the cause of sickness or health issues. The book of Proverbs says, "A merry heart does good, like medicine" (Proverbs 17:22, NKJV). So a merry thought is a happy thought which produces a good emotion that, in return, produces healing neuropeptides that circulate in your body, going to every cell and every cell's receptor. Negative thoughts are producing a toxic neuropeptide that is circulating in your body and going to every cell and every cell's receptor.

The last three years of our lives have been very challenging, to say the least. We have seen pestilence and disease in our world in a way that we thought we would never see in our lifetime. We have seen racial and social injustice emerge in a way that we believed was many years behind us, only to find out that it is very much alive. We have seen catastrophic disasters like wildfires raging in the hills of California, earthquakes, locust swarms, mudslides, floods, war in Ukraine, etc. The year 2020 proved to be one of the deadliest in which to be alive, and these past two years of COVID-19 have kept everyone at the edge of their seats, waiting for what is to come next.

---

14 Candace B. Pert, PhD, *Molecules of Emotion: Why You Feel the Way You Feel* (New York: Scribner, 2003).

This greatly challenges our ability to live in a peaceful state. This is why we must be able to control our thoughts. If we don't, as stated before, our subconscious will give us supporting thoughts for every thought that we have, and if we follow that path, it could possibly be one of absolutely no peace at all.

Just as the waves function in the capacity for which they were created and never deviate from it, just as the sun—whenever called upon by the orders of creation—brings its radiant light and illumination to the world, we are obligated to do the same. We, the ultimate creation, have a responsibility and a mandate from God to be all that He created us to be. However, it is interesting that we, out of all of His creations, are enormously challenged at taking a rightful position and just being who He created us to be.

CHAPTER 3

PICTURE THIS

A s I sat down to write, I thought about having taken my morning walk on the beach. I had noticed that there were footprints already on the sand. At the same time I was making footprints, I couldn't help but notice that all of the other footprints were different. This gave me clear imagery to note the fact that we each make our own individual footprint in the sand . . . and in the world. Sadly, many times the footprints that we leave are not the footprints of the real us because we have, from birth, been given a program that created in us a false sense of identity.

It is by design that we are all so very different. Some of the footprints were wide, some of them were slim, some of them were neat, and some of them were not so neat, but they made an imprint. Therefore, as individuals, we must learn how to appreciate our individuality. It would be a sad thing to walk through the course of life, not considering the fact that you are leaving an imprint. The beauty of it is that you and I have a choice. We can decide what imprint we choose to leave.

WHEN OUR CREATOR MADE US, HE MADE US FREE WILL MORAL AGENTS. HE GAVE US THE RIGHT TO CHOOSE AND MAKE OUR OWN DECISIONS. YES, THERE IS A PATH THAT HE HAS CHARTED OUT FOR US, BUT WE HAVE THE ABILITY TO CHOOSE THAT PATH OR ANOTHER PATH.

I would like for us to take a look at imagination and visualization and discover the similarities and differences.

According to *Webster's Dictionary*, the definition of visualization is "the formation of mental visual images"[15]; the definition of imagination, however, is "the act or power of forming a mental image of something . . . never before perceived in reality."[16]

Visualization involves forming a picture in your mind. It is the practice of imagining what you want to achieve in the future. This mental picture is usually something we have already seen. It also involves many of your senses: touch, smell, sight, sound, and taste, also feelings. You can imagine things that you have never seen.

15 "Visualization Definition & Meaning," *Merriam-Webster*, Merriam-Webster, https://www.merriam-webster.com/dictionary/visualization.
16 "Imagination Definition & Meaning," *Merriam-Webster*, Merriam-Webster, https://www.merriam-webster.com/dictionary/imagination.

The daily practice of visualizing your dreams can help you to reach your goals faster:

» **It activates your creative subconscious** which will start generating creative ideas to achieve your goals.[17]

» **It programs your brain** to recognize the resources you will need to achieve your dreams.

» **It builds your internal** impulse to take the necessary actions to achieve your dreams.[18]

How do you visualize something? Get comfortable, close your eyes, and imagine—in as vivid detail as you can—what you would be looking at if the dream you have were already realized. Imagine looking at the ideal result.

Visualizing believes something will happen, whereas fantasizing is dreaming about something you lack that you don't believe you will ever achieve. It can lead you to dwell on what you don't have rather than motivate you to work to achieve it.

Is visualization the same as daydreaming? No, daydreaming is a natural ability; images come and go as they please, often without any logical connection. Visualization, however, is not random.

17 "The Power of Visualization to Manifestation," *Brains on Walls*, 21 May 2020, https://www.brainsonwalls.com/the-power-of-visualization-to-manifestation/.
18 Jack Canfield, "Visualization Techniques to Manifest Desired Outcomes," *Jack Canfield*, 9 Aug. 2022, https://jackcanfield.com/blog/visualize-and-affirm-your-desired-outcomes-a-step-by-step-guide/.

It's not unexpected. It is done with a definite purpose or goal in mind before you begin.

My mother and father taught me how to dream; they were programming me and didn't even realize it. My father was very entrepreneurial-minded and had several small businesses. In the process of my studies, I began to reflect upon my years with my parents. While they were not super successful in their entrepreneurial endeavors, I can clearly see that it was their influence and impartation that set me on the path that I now choose to walk. Growing up, I remember family businesses and countless hours being spent working on and developing them. My father was very focused and diligent whenever he had an idea and would work it until the very end. I so vividly remember, night after night, sitting with my mother as she would go through catalogs dreaming of what she was going to purchase. I also remember making her promises that once I got older, I would make some of these purchases for her, and just in case you're wondering, yes, I did follow through with my promise.

I can also remember coming home from school, getting homework done, and sitting with her watching her soap operas. There was this one show in particular that she just had to watch—*The Young and the Restless*. On that show, there was a character named Victor Newman, and Victor always seemed to be able to work out any family situation or dilemma. One of the things that stood out the most to me was his love and care for his family. During the summer, he would gather them all and take them to their summer home to retreat. Seeing and hearing this created a desire in me to have a summer home. This made an impression on me, and I looked at my mother and said to her, "One day, we will have a summer home."

My faith partnered with my hope and my imagination, and my summer home was manifested years later. It was not something that I talked about a lot, but it was always imprinted within the confines of my subconscious mind. There were times I mentioned it to other people, and they laughed, which was discouraging, but there's something about the imagination that can create such a place of reality that it becomes impossible to let it go. We must limit who we share our dreams with because, in many instances, they only create a chasm that becomes difficult for most relationships to overcome.

Imagination is something that is not seen, and most people cannot connect to what they cannot see. Perhaps it is time for you to change your surroundings to a new group of people that have like vision of a greater future. If you want to kill a big dream, tell it to a small-minded person. If you don't believe me, ask Joseph from the Bible. He told his dream to his brothers, they could not see it, and then—literally—they tried to kill him.

IMAGINATION IS SOMETHING THAT IS NOT SEEN, AND MOST PEOPLE CANNOT CONNECT TO WHAT THEY CANNOT SEE.

That day, when I walked the beach, which was about a five-mile stretch from my condo, I saw many seashells along the way. I noticed that there were dead creatures—like a jellyfish—that had washed up on the shore. I got a little fatigued, but I kept walking. The thought crossed my mind to turn around and go back, but voices deep within me (subconscious) said, *Just keep walking, and you will get there.* So I just kept walking.

When I got to the pier, there was a sign that said, "No pets allowed!" Sometimes, the people who walk with you to the pier can't go out on the pier with you. Sometimes, we get discouraged and depressed when someone walks out or stops being a part of our lives. You have to remember that everyone is not equipped to go the distance with you. Some people are in your life for a season, and some are there for a lifetime. Trying to hold on to seasonal people can stunt your growth and delay your destiny. Many times, we know it's time to let go of an individual, but there is something deep inside of us that wants to hold on. I also noticed that there was a fee that had to be paid to walk out on the pier. You must understand that there is a price to be paid to walk in the life that you desire to walk. The question is this: are you willing to pay the price?

I was barefoot because I had been walking on the beach. I started towards the pier after paying the fee, and a lady stopped me and said, "Do you have shoes?" She further stated, "The only way you can walk on the pier, even though you have paid the price, is you must wear shoes." The purpose of the shoes is to avoid any hooks and nails protruding from the floor of the pier that could hurt me. So even though the pier was beautiful, there were still challenges to walking it. We, as individuals, must understand that even though the life we desire, the relationship we desire, or the career we desire may be beautiful, there will always be challenges that we must overcome in order to enjoy what we are desiring.

I noticed as I got further out on the pier that there were additional signs: "No shark fishing," "Only 2 poles per person," and other rules. We tend to think that if we reach a certain place—a certain status—in life, we are exempt from rules. It doesn't matter how high you go; there will always be rules and regulations that you will have to abide by. So the purpose of gaining status and wealth, prosperity and position, should never be to see yourself above other people. There will always be a governing body that's over you.

From my starting point, the pier was freshly built. It seemed to have countless benches along the way that you could stop and sit on to enjoy the view of the beautiful ocean. The ocean seemed endless. It was like you could just walk forever and never run out of pier.

IT DOESN'T MATTER HOW HIGH YOU GO; THERE WILL ALWAYS BE RULES AND REGULATIONS THAT YOU WILL HAVE TO ABIDE BY.

As I walked a little bit further, I noticed another sign that listed fishing regulations and gave insight as to the different species that you could catch and keep. It even provided instructions on how to measure a fish once you'd caught it. This made me think about the further need for instructions as we reach certain pinnacles in life. Once you attain a certain amount of success in your walk, you need instruction as to how to handle as well as maintain the success.

I looked down at the wristband I had been given and realized it signified that I had paid the price to walk the pier. People that walk the pier of success ALL bear a mark that signifies the fact that they have paid the price to walk where they are walking. So don't despise your process, for it is the process that pays the price for the walk out on the pier.

LOOKING AT MILES AND MILES OF BEACH SHORE REMINDS ME THAT LIFE IS FULL OF ENDLESS POSSIBILITIES AND OPPORTUNITIES.

I was snapped out of my reverie as I looked at my watch and realized that I had been writing for four hours. At the same time, I noticed that the beach was becoming crowded and full. When I had started my writing, there were few people out on the beach. In the four hours I had been working on my dream, the other people had been perhaps sleeping. The dream, the mission, or the promise has to be worth getting up early to get ahead of the sleepers. You can sleep and get a dream, but you cannot sleep and fulfill the dream.

Thinking back to the miles and miles of washed-up jellyfish along the shore, I realized they had been pushed out of their element by the tide. It is crucial that your mind be grounded in a force that will anchor and sustain you through the currents of life. Understand that, in order to obtain success, you must become grounded in something or the current of life—the tides of life—will force you out of your element.

The main thing that you need is to be grounded in a relationship with Christ. There is no greater anchor, form of stability, or place of refuge and safety than in Him. Dr. Myles Monroe is quoted as saying, "If you seek to know the purpose of a thing, you must go to the creator of the thing." The apostle Paul put it this way: "In him we live and move and have our being" (Acts 17:28, NIV). If we are ever to be grounded and one with ourselves, we must first be one with the Creator who made us.

The road to success is not just for us to walk alone; we must take someone else with us. My wife, Deloris, and I were in Aruba, and we decided to go parasailing. Our boat stopped to pick up another group, and in this group was a mother and her son. They both were terrified because they had never parasailed before. Deloris and I began to console them. We said, "It's going to be a great experience!"

The little boy, who was about eight, said to us, "So, what is it like?"

What we decided to do was to cast a vision for him of the ride of his life. I began to tell him he would feel like a superhero flying through the air. I knew that most every kid loves superheroes. They dream of being a superhero. I said to him, "When you get up there, just spread your arms out, and let your cape blow in the wind just like Superman."

My wife told him, "Then, look to the right, and you will see people riding banana boats and jet skis. You'll be flying above them all, and when you look to the left, you will see your hotel."

What we were doing was casting vision for him to take his mind off of the anxiety and put it on the possibility that he could really enjoy the ride. Needless to say, he did. He came back down ecstatic, jumping around, saying that it was the best thing that he had ever done in his life.

What is it? What is that thing that you have been desiring to do, but anxiety has you too afraid to step out and do it? We become so paralyzed by the "What if?" that we fail to step out and try. I'm reminded of the lyrics to a song:

> "...There's a dream out there
> With your name on it."[19]

19 Jennifer Holliday, vocalist, "A Dream With Your Name On It," by Bonnie Karlyle and Tom Lerner, released November 11, 1991, track 4 on *I'm On Your Side*, Arista Records, Inc.

Close your eyes, and begin to imagine the feeling of success. Imagine yourself soaring like my wife and I and this little guy and his mother did as we parasailed. Imagine the wind beneath your arms as you stretch them out, walking in destiny. Imagine soaring above thousands of people who are too afraid to walk in their dream. Imagine even the possibility of being able to come down and help some of those people realize their dream. Imagine how the world would be a better place if you saw the fulfillment of your dream, and your dream was able to bring fulfillment to someone else's dream.

Imagine the invention that you have been sitting on for years changing the course of the world. Perhaps, it could be the one thing that takes us from riding in cars to flying through the air. You then would be listed among the greats, such as the Wright brothers who invented the concept of the airplane. Perhaps, you have the passion, the drive, the insight, and the intuition that Dr. Martin Luther King, Jr. had living inside of you. Perhaps, God could use you to start the next movement for racial and social equality, uniting the people of the world from all races, colors, and creeds as one body, serving one God.

The chair that you are sitting in as you read this book was created by someone. The AirPods that you are wearing as you listen to this audiobook were created by someone. The glasses that you wear to be able to see the print in this book . . . they were, one day, just a thought in someone's mind.

May I suggest to you that somewhere deeply embedded within your subconscious mind is a great invention, and if you could learn to harness the thoughts of your subconscious mind, you could be the next great inventor? Connected to your subconscious mind is the infinite power of the Creator—a Creator who stepped out of eternity into time and said to time, "Let there be. . ." and everything He said, we experience the benefit of today.

CONNECTED TO YOUR SUBCONSCIOUS MIND IS THE INFINITE POWER OF THE CREATOR—A CREATOR WHO STEPPED OUT OF ETERNITY INTO TIME AND SAID TO TIME, "LET THERE BE. . ." AND EVERYTHING HE SAID, WE EXPERIENCE THE BENEFIT OF TODAY.

WHAT IF ...

What if I told you that the income you earned last year . . . you have the potential of doubling it this year?

_____

_____

What if I told you that the prognosis you got from the doctor was just an opportunity for you to see the greatest miracle you have ever seen in your life?

_____

_____

What if I told you that the body you have been longing for can absolutely be yours? All you have to do is lock in and focus, and you will experience body transformation.

_____

_____

CHAPTER 4

HOW DO YOU RESET?

n an article titled "Self Mastery: A Complete Guide to Actualizing Your Potential," Scott Jeffrey states:

Although many of us refuse the call to adventure, developing our innate capacities is our destiny. Fighting this destiny brings depression and anxiety. Embracing it leads to freedom and fulfillment. We all have an intrinsic motivation toward growth.[20]

Something pushes us, driving us to level-up. When we look at life, Jeffrey says, we find self-actualizing people in virtually every field of interest: business professionals, artists, musicians, philosophers, painters, doctors, psychologists, athletes, and martial artists.[21] Be one of them!

Walking back from the pier, I looked down at the beautiful sand under my feet and decided to draw. Yes, because I could. There was no reason I couldn't. I was not in a hurry. I was not on a schedule, and the creative me wanted to draw in the sand just

20 Scott Jeffrey, "Self Mastery: A Complete Guide to Actualizing Your Potential," *Scott Jeffrey*, 18 Feb. 2020, https://scottjeffrey.com/self-mastery/#:~:text=Self%20mastery%20is%20often%20defined,will%20to%20 realize%20that%20vision.
21 Scott Jeffrey, "Self Mastery: A Complete Guide to Actualizing Your Potential."

because I could. Sometimes, you should get rid of the schedule and stop. Do it because it's what you want to do.

PAUSE FOR A MOMENT, GO INSIDE OF YOUR MIND, AND HARNESS THE DREAM, THE GOAL, THAT YOU'VE LONGED FOR BUT HAVE BEEN TOO BUSY TO STOP AND DRAW IT OUT.

What is it that you want to do? Let's pause for a moment, go inside of your mind, and harness the dream, the goal, that you've longed for but have been too busy to stop and draw it out. Is it time for you to stop the procrastination and just do it? If you don't, how will you feel five years from now? How long will you allow self-sabotaging programs that have been embedded deep within your subconscious mind to control your destiny?

So, I drew a huge circle. Inside the circle, I put my name. Then, I began to draw lines. Each of those lines represented endless possibilities in my life. Understand that your world can only be as large as you can see it. I drew a large circle because I see great things coming to my life. The size of the circle represented the frequency or the magnitude of the energy that I choose to generate in my world because the frequency that you put out is the frequency you will receive. The lines in the circle represented the things that I will accomplish—dreams that I must achieve. And of course, I'm sure you know that the circle represented the world that I live in. For me, looking at the circle, all I could see were endless possibilities and unlimited potential. What do you see in your circle? If you only see where you are right now, then your possibilities are limited. You need a reset.

My purpose in sharing my location as I wrote this book is to help you tap into your visualization skills because imagination is everything. It's the key to life's coming attractions. You must be able to visualize yourself in the future in order to get to the future that you desire. So just take a moment, close your eyes, and see yourself in the future. See yourself actually doing the thing that brings you the most fulfillment—doing the thing that you could do and be happy even if there were no compensation attached. How does it feel? What does it look like?

I wrote from a city that exudes life and creativity—a city that's blazing with neon lights. It's full of people who are creative, presenting their talents on stages that are filled with every kind of entertainment that you could imagine, with themes ranging from hotels that represent cities to hotels that represent movies to hotels that represent countries. This city never sleeps. The weather that day was 107 °F, and I realized that all that I saw and experienced had been—one day—just a thought in someone's mind. I got to sit there and enjoy the manifestation of what was once in their minds because they literally made the thought become a reality.

As I sat out by the pool surrounded by people from all walks of life, they all seemed to have the attitude and persona, *We are all here for a common goal. Let's get to know each other a little and enjoy these days before we have to go back to our everyday lives.* Serenity and solidarity produce a chemical in your body that, when released, will cause you to live longer, be happy, and enjoy life more.

I decided to take a swim. When I came back to my spot, the sun had moved. I wanted to be in the shade, so I picked up my things and moved to another spot where there was a gentleman lying a few rows away from me. I decided to sit in the shade and began to write about the principles that you are reading in this book. After a while, two ladies came out of nowhere and began to engage me in conversation. We shared where we were from and how long we would be in the city. Then, they inquired what I was writing about, and I told them the concept of my book. I explained the difference between the conscious and the subconscious mind, the powers that lie within the subconscious mind, and how the subconscious mind is always working to manifest what we believe.

They began to share with me the story of their brother who was sitting two chairs away. They expressed to me that he had been in an accident, and as a result of the accident, he suffered memory loss. He was having difficulty with relationships in the family as well as trouble on his job as a result of becoming withdrawn due to the trauma of the accident.

After talking with them for about forty-five minutes, they engaged their brother in the conversation. Nick began to express to me the sentiments of his heart as they related to where he was in life and what the changes had brought about. I immediately began to talk with Nick about inner healing, and I shared with him that his thought processes had everything to do with the restoration of his mind; I also shared with him that our body was designed and created to heal itself, and anything outside of that goes against the original plan and design for the body. I asked Nick if he believed it, and he said yes. I then proceeded to ask Nick what his desire was for his current situation. Nick said that he desired to have his full memory back and be able to, once again, lead a normal life.

I had recently been given a good read titled *The Power of Your Subconscious Mind* written by Dr. Joseph Murphy.[22] In his book, Dr. Murphy shared countless stories he had recorded of people being healed simply because they believed; belief has power. A study was conducted on a certain group of people given a medication that was supposed to bring about healing in their body. Another group of people was given a placebo. The results of the study proved to be extremely enlightening as they related to the concept of belief in the power of the subconscious mind.

THE SUBCONSCIOUS MIND DOES NOT HAVE THE ABILITY TO DECIPHER BETWEEN REALITY AND IMAGINATION.

22 Joseph Murphy, PhD, DD, *The Power of Your Subconscious Mind* (Santa Fe, NM: Martino Publishing, 2011).

In the study, a great number of the people given the placebo were healed, and it was simply because of their belief in the medication they were given. The subconscious mind does not have the ability to decipher between reality and imagination; therefore, when they were given the placebo, their conscious mind believed that it was the medication and began to work with the thought that it could heal the body. We must understand that with whatever we take into our minds, we are writing a software program that will eventually become hardwired in our brains and produce some type of fruit.

Remember that what you write on the inside, you will experience on the outside. What are you writing? As we talked, I began to see Nick's countenance change. He went from being slumped over to sitting up straight. His eyes became brighter, and his voice inflection changed to that of great excitement. Nick, for the first time since his traumatic experience, was beginning to see something different. It was obvious to me that Nick was downloading the information that could put him on the path to a reset. I would say that my vacation time spent with Nick out by the pool was purposeful and time well-spent.

However, I am not sure if it was more impactful for me or for Nick because I left him with an even greater passion to share this knowledge with the world. There are so many people like Nick who just need to know that whatever the state or condition they are in, there's hope. And in many instances, the hope that you need lies deep within you. In the movie version of *The Voyage of the Dawn Treader*, one of the Chronicles of Narnia books written by

C. S. Lewis, one of the characters says, "Hardship often prepares ordinary people for extraordinary destinies."[23]

We have all been given a divine gift from God. It's the one thing that you do with great efficiency and with the least amount of effort. If you live in the gift that God gave you, it will change your life and the lives of all that you encounter.

WHAT IF . . .

What if I told you that if you'll change your belief system and begin to process your life through the lens of "I can" instead of "I can't," your world would be transformed in twenty-four hours?

_____

_____

What if I told you the house that you've been dreaming of is just what God wants to give you, and the only thing standing between it and you is you taking charge of the power of your subconscious mind?

_____

_____

23 William O'Flaherty, "(CCSLQ-2) We Read to Know" *Essential C.S. Lewis*, 5 Sept. 2015, https://essentialcslewis.com/2015/09/05/we-read-to-know/.

What if I told you that every negative thing that you have suffered had left you with a gift, but you have just not been focused enough to see it?

_____

_____

CHAPTER 5

MASTER OF ONE

To change your state of mind, you have to change your physiology. Physiology includes the way you move, the way you breathe, and your facial expressions. Your body posture and movements help to determine the way you feel, so emotion is created by motion.

I asked earlier what you would say if I told you that even though you've had great success in your life and experienced genuine love, peace, and joy, that the best days of your life are still to come.

Did you wonder, *How could that be?*

The answer is really very simple: You must learn how to take control of your assets. You must learn how to master your perception. You must learn how to take ownership of the part of you that controls your emotions, your will, and ultimately your actions—the subconscious you!

I CHALLENGE YOU—I BESEECH YOU—I IMPLORE YOU— TO GIVE YOURSELF THE GIFT OF SELF-MASTERY.

So today, I challenge you—I beseech you—I implore you—to *give yourself the gift of self-mastery.*

Say this with me:

"I can."
"I will."
"I must."

Scott Jeffrey, in his article titled "Self Mastery: A Complete Guide to Actualizing Your Potential," states:

> *Self mastery is defined by self-control, the ability to exert a strong will against our impulses to steer our future to one of our choosing. But this is only one aspect of the term. Self mastery requires being able to visualize yourself in the future and harnessing the will to realize that vision.*[24]

This becomes very challenging for many people because when confronted by life, it is difficult for individuals to see beyond their current circumstances. This is when everyone must rely on a deep inner sense of peace and power, understanding that the infinite force that is embedded within our subconscious mind (God) is silently working all things together for our good.

Jeffrey goes on to say, "We learn to master ourselves by getting out of our own way. We strip away what we are not, in order to realize

---

24 Scott Jeffrey, "Self Mastery: A Complete Guide to Actualizing Your Potential," *Scott Jeffrey*, 18 Feb. 2020, https://scottjeffrey.com/self-mastery/#:~:text=Self%20mastery%20is%20often%20defined,will%20to%20realize%20that%20vision.

who and what we really are, actualizing [or making a reality of] our potential in the process."[25] If we are ever going to be who He created us to be, we must be delivered from the self-defeating belief systems that keep us bound and going around in circles. Our greatest deliverance will be from SELF.

What if I told you that the you that you think you are is not really you? Instead, you are the sum total of the programs that were given to you for the first seven years of your life. However, if you practice the principles of self-mastery and work through the process, you can become the greatest expression of you that has ever walked the face of the earth.

True success is when you learn how to live your life in a way that you can experience an enormous amount of pleasure and joy in spite of your circumstances. Learning to control your subconscious mind will enable you to do that. Remember: You are the authority. You have dominion in your own life. What you desire to see in the world, you must create. The Creator is in you; therefore, there is no lack of creativity in your biological makeup because you were made in His image and likeness, and everything about Him speaks to creative power. Take the attitude that you refuse to let the habits of your past stop you from this transformation.

This metamorphosis is also referred to by the apostle Paul in Romans 12:2. In this text, Paul was in conversation with the Roman church, encouraging them to be transformed by the renewing of their minds (reset). They had begun to allow their

---

25 Scott Jeffrey, "A Complete Guide to Actualizing Your Potential."

external environment to affect their spirituality, and Paul was trying to get them to understand that the patterns of the world should neither control their thought processes nor their actions. In order to be something other than what they saw in their external environment, they had to take control of their thoughts.

The metaphor that I would like to use to help us understand what Paul was sharing is that of a butterfly. The butterfly starts out as a microscopic egg. That's its state of being, and through nature's processes and time, it's changed into another state of being which is a caterpillar. You would never know that the caterpillar came from a microscopic egg because it's totally different. Then, through process and time, the caterpillar is encased by a cocoon; that state of being came from something that looked like a worm. Finally, through process and time, it goes into another state of being which is a butterfly. It starts as a microscopic egg, but it's transformed. It evolves according to its intention. In the infinite wisdom of God, He created everything for a purpose: birds to fly in the air, fish to swim in the sea, and humanity to manage it all. And in this, we see the beauty of life—the beauty of diversity.

However, Paul was saying it's like that with us. He said, "[B]e ye transformed by the renewing of your mind" (Romans 12:2, KJV). What that means is that you are in this state of being, and in order to move to a better state of being, you have to renew your mind. Let's say you start out as a negative, critical, judgmental person—that's your state of being. To evolve into a person who doesn't judge and criticize, your thinking has to be renewed. *Be ye transformed by the renewing of your mind.*

Now, you may have eliminated being critical and judgmental, but you may be letting your thoughts boss you, and you may have unforgiveness. By the renewing of your mind, you can move from that state of being to no criticism . . . no judgment . . . *and* walking in forgiveness. Paul says that just like a butterfly, you—as an individual—can be transformed from one state of being to another state of being. You have to have your mind renewed—reset—or you cannot evolve into a better state of being.

IN ORDER TO RENEW YOUR MIND, YOU HAVE TO BOSS YOUR THOUGHTS INSTEAD OF ALLOWING THEM TO BOSS YOU.

In order to renew your mind, you have to boss your thoughts instead of allowing them to boss you, and that's done by reading materials that deal with thinking correctly. You have to set an intention that you're not going to be a person of critical judgment or a gossiper. You really have to work on your mind because that's where thoughts are—everything starts with a thought. This is why we must continually guard our gates. They are the entryway to our souls, and it is through them that good or evil enters our minds.

It is time for a brand new you. Get excited at the possibility of change. Embrace the desire to evolve. You must be passionate about getting up off the ground and soaring with the eagles. You've got to be tired of doing what you've always done because if you do what you've always done, you'll always be where you've always been. You must have the attitude that says, *I know for sure I am destined for success, and everything I put my hands to is going to work.* Understand that the real battle is in your mind; the war, the fight, is between the waking mind and the sleeping mind. It is a fight that you must win if you are going to evolve into the best version of you. Your greatest accomplishment will be getting the victory over what you think about yourself and what you say about yourself. You will never be defeated by what other people say about you, but you are defeated by what you say about you. So what are you saying?

Since applying these principles and concepts to my life, my perception has changed. I see things from a different vantage point. My thought process is different. When I wake up in the morning and look in the mirror, I see different. I wake up with a greater sense of expectation, understanding that there's a world full of opportunity that's waiting for me to claim what is rightfully mine—to step out on a world full of promise, understanding that it's my time to rise! I will rise above whatever has been standing in my way, the negative belief system that I have carried all my life, and all of the negative criticism that has told me that I can't. I must rise up and become the greatest, fullest, and grandest expression of me.

IF JESUS WANTS ME TO LIVE, I CHOOSE TO LIVE—ABOVE FAITHLESSNESS AND INSECURITY, IN MY PRESENT INSTEAD OF MY PAST, AND IN A WORLD THAT I CHOOSE TO DESIGN!

It's time for you and me to realize that we are a city that has been set upon a hill and cannot be hidden (Matthew 5:15). The world is waiting for the greatness that's down inside you! According to the Word, it's your time to shine! Shine above social injustice, above a belief system that seeks to hold you down, above your haters and naysayers, and above the darkness of this world that seeks to hold you and others in captivity. Tell yourself confidently: *It's my time to live! Jesus said that He came that I might have life and life more abundantly* (John 10:10). *So if He wants me to live, I choose to live—above faithlessness and insecurity, in my present instead of my past, and in a world that I choose to design! It's my time to fly above the pressures of life that try to control my mind—above fear, doubt, and disbelief—out of my now and into my tomorrow!*

If you believe that it's your time, and you're ready to walk in it, shout: "It's my time. It's my time!"

CHAPTER 6

FAITH-COLORED GLASSES

C hanging the way we represent things to ourselves—the way we picture things in our head—is one way that we focus. Albert Einstein said, "Imagination is more important than knowledge. Knowledge is limited. Imagination encircles the world." [26] So you must begin to dream, to think, and to imagine what the next season of your life is going to be like.

My question to you is this: What do you see in your future? The Bible says that we have the ability to "call those things that be not as though they are, and they will manifest. According to your faith/belief be it unto you" (Romans 4:17, author paraphrase). This is a promise. So what are you going to do with this promise? Are you going to believe it, act on it, and allow it to come to full fruition in your life? Or are you going to stay where you are, doing what you've always done and getting the same results?

YOU CAN HAVE THE LIFE THAT YOU DREAM ABOUT. ALL YOU HAVE TO DO IS BE WILLING TO TRUST THE PROCESS, PUT THE TIME IN, AND DO THE WORK.

26 Annabel Acton, "10 Einstein Quotes to Fire up Your Creativity," *Inc.*, 4 Oct. 2017, https://www.inc.com/annabel-acton/10-einstein-quotes-to-fire-up-your-creativity.html.

I hope it's not the latter. You don't have to; you can have the life that you dream about. All you have to do is be willing to trust the process, put the time in, and do the work. You will see the manifestation of what you have been dreaming of. Another scripture (Jeremiah 29:11, author paraphrase) says, "For I know that I have for you plans to give you a hope and a future, plans to prosper you." And this is in every area of your life: career, health, relationships, and finances. Understand that when our Creator makes this kind of promise, He has the power, the ability, and the wherewithal to make good on it.

WHAT IF . . .

What if I told you that the only thing standing between you and the best season of your life is you getting up and moving in the direction of the thing you've been hoping for?

_____

_____

CHAPTER 7

HARNESS YOUR THOUGHTS

nother way we take charge of our thoughts is by what we say to ourselves. If we change what we say, we can change how we feel.

Are you ready to change your state?

Are you ready to change your world?

Are you ready to make your mark?

If you're ready, say, "Yes."

If you're willing, say, "Yes."

If you refuse to let anyone stop you, say, "Yes."

And if your sanity depends on it, say, "Yes!"

The number one breakthrough for all leaders is constant, never-ending improvement. That means educating yourself and connecting yourself with individuals who are doing what you want to do—networking.

Tony Robbins says that our number one problem in life is not a problem of resources. It is a problem of resourcefulness![27]

Lasting success is continuing to develop even greater emotional mastery because that's what affects whether you execute or not. The opportunity for self-education and self-knowledge is there!

We have to change our psychology from, *I'm going to do what everybody else does, and I'm mad because it doesn't work anymore!* to the reality of, *This is that the greatest time to be alive if I'm growing, learning, developing, and educating myself with valuable skills.* So instead of complaining, you've got to say to yourself, *What and where are the skill sets valued in the marketplace? And how do I work harder on myself than anyone else, because if I become more valuable than the rest, I will be able to give more and do more and change more.*

Are you ready to go to the next level?

Are you ready to live your best life NOW?

Are you ready to see the best version of yourself that has ever been?

THERE ARE NO JUSTIFIED RESENTMENTS.

---

27 Tony Robbins, "The Ultimate Resource Is Resourcefulness—Tony Robbins Quote," *Tony Robbins Quotes*, 2 Dec. 2020, https://tonyrobbinsquotes.com/the-ultimate-resource-is-resourcefulness/.

Can I suggest to you that one of the things holding you back from becoming just that is the resentment that you are holding onto from your past? Remember: You cannot go into your future while holding on to your past. We tend to do that because they wronged us—we're JUSTIFIED!

There are no justified resentments. You carry around resentment inside of you toward someone who has hurt you or wronged you in the past or owes you money—toward the person that was abusive to you, walked out on you, and left you. I've heard Bishop T.D. Jakes put it this way: Anybody that can walk out of your life . . . let them go! Because anyone that is meant to be a part of your future can't just walk away. You only need people with you who have the ability to stick with you through the thick and thin, the ups and downs, and the ins and outs—understanding that there may be more outs than ins, but it's all taking us to a destination. I'm speaking to all of the things that you have justified in your heart and concluded that you have a right to be angry over, I am suggesting to you that those things will only end up harming you and creating in you a great sense of despair.

It is often said that no one ever dies from a snake bite. It is the venom that keeps pouring through your body after the bite that will, oftentimes, kill you. To fight this, you have to be willing to take responsibility for whatever is going on in your life and decide not to give your power to others. In some instances, you have to be willing to say, "I am here because of the choices I made." Take the attitude of no blame. This is where you start to embrace the concept of no justified resentments.

Can I share a personal story?

I was a part of a corporation for years, and in this corporation, the CEO became like a father to me. He began to mentor me—take me into his home with his family as a son—which was awesome. It gave me a great sense of validation and self-worth. Looking back on this, he must have been able to see the potential for greatness inside of me.

He went to great lengths to make sure that I understood things like once you move into the eye of the public, everything that you do is scrutinized. There were conversations such as the importance of choosing the right companion with the right appearance because this could determine the social environments that you would be accepted in—even down to considering your children, their mental capacities, and their physical appearance. These are all things that should be considered as you pursue advancing in your life and sharing it with someone else, and they proved to be of great value to me.

While I don't believe that there is that *one* magical perfect person, I do believe that if we consider these aspects as we are searching for companionship, they will aid us in having long and fruitful relationships. Having been married now for thirty-five years, I am sure that it was some of these principles applied at the beginning that have helped me sustain healthy relationships. You see, two individuals must have some of the same goals and interests to keep them engaged in each other's life.

There were conversations about investing in the proper things in life so that I could get the proper return; however, the moment I decided to pursue a career outside of the family business, everything changed. It all went south, as they say . . . shut down. I became a castoff, and for me, it was like a dagger being placed in my heart. This man was my lifeline. I remember getting up in the morning and looking in the mirror and wishing I could look just like him—as a son would his father. He represented the epitome of everything I ever wanted. He was a man that loved and fully embraced his family as well as his career.

But it all changed in one moment, leading me to a place of despair and hopelessness and having to fight emotions that I had never imagined having to feel or fight as it related to this man that I saw in my heart as Dad. I was publicly humiliated, banned from the company, and left for dead. I did, however, receive validation from higher officials in the company, but none of it could soothe the pain in my heart of being rejected by the man that I saw as Dad.

Many times, our greatest pain is caused by the people that we love the most, the people closest to us. Even though I was released from the company and excelled in other companies, there was still a sense of wanting his approval for everything I did, perhaps even waiting for a surprise phone call in which he would say, "Hey, I've been watching from afar, and I'm proud of your accomplishments," only to be disappointed year after year. Finally, one day, I was in a conversation with a friend, and he said to me, "That may never happen. You have to let it go, move on, and begin to celebrate your own success."

That proved to be one of the most liberating moments of my life. It was like a light came on, an "aha" moment, and I began to process my life from that moment on through a different set of lenses, realizing that the true measure of success is not found in how others see us. It's how we view ourselves and our accomplishments. Once again, this presented an opportunity for me to take control of my thoughts and my emotions and change my outcome. This was, for sure, a reset.

THE TRUE MEASURE OF SUCCESS IS NOT FOUND IN HOW OTHERS SEE US. IT'S HOW WE VIEW OURSELVES AND OUR ACCOMPLISHMENTS.

Some years later, I took it upon myself to reach out and visit with the man I saw as Dad. The conversation left me with one of the greatest wisdom nuggets that has ever blessed my life. After pouring my heart out to him, he looked at me, sat back in his chair, and said to me, "You know how we know that we have honestly forgiven someone?" With great enthusiasm, I said to him, "How?" And he said to me, "When you can look that individual in the face and not feel the pain that you felt in the situation, you have genuinely forgiven." This was a moment in time that I will never, ever forget, and I use it in my counseling sessions with my clients. If you do the work and the process of inner healing on yourself, forgiveness becomes possible, and you can live your life free of the pain of unforgiveness. In order to create a brighter future, you must crush, destroy, and annihilate all of the limiting beliefs that are living in your head.

As I started my writing journey in a city that was fully equipped to give me all the inspiration I needed, it was approximately 97 °F, and the sun was shining all around me as I sat on my deck, overlooking the pool. People were everywhere. The pool was surrounded by a lazy river that extended for at least five miles. Outside of the pool was a lake with a beautiful fountain in the middle. Behind the lake was a beautiful golf course, beyond which stretched miles and miles of beautiful trees. The feeling that I got as I gazed out into the distance was one of peace and tranquility. All that I experienced in that city was just, one day, a thought in someone's mind that became a wonderful reality that I had the pleasure of enjoying. Albert Einstein is also quoted as saying, "Imagination is everything. It is the preview of life's coming attractions."[28]

WHAT IF . . .

What if you decided that the dream inside of you has the potential to create a whole new world for someone else to enjoy?

_____

_____

28 Louise Myers, "36 Famous Albert Einstein Quotes That Will Blow Your Mind," *Louise Myers Visual Social Media*, 25 Aug. 2021, https://louisem.com/64476/famous-einstein-quotes#:~:text=Albert%20Einstein%20 quotes%20on%20imagination,-Logic%20will%20get&text=Imagination%20is%20everything.,draw%20 freely%20upon%20my%20imagination.

What if you made a choice to wholeheartedly pursue your life's passion?

_____

_____

What if money were not an issue, and education were not a factor? What would you be doing?

_____

_____

CHAPTER 8

ONLY BELIEVE

I t is an awesome thing that God has given us the ability to create the life that we want to live. So my question is this: What kind of life are you living? Is it the life that you desire to live? If it is not, why isn't it when God has given us the right to create? And if it is not the life that you desire, what are you willing to invest to make it the life that you want?

WE CREATE WHAT WE BELIEVE, UNDERSTANDING THAT THOUGHT FUSED WITH FEELINGS BECOMES A SUBJECTIVE FAITH OR BELIEF.

Remember: Henry Ford put forth the idea that those who say they can and those who say they can't are both right. We create what we believe, understanding that thought fused with feelings becomes a subjective faith or belief, and, "According to your belief be it done to you" (Matthew 9:29, ESV).

MY HOSPITAL STORY

One evening while driving in the suburbs of Atlanta, Georgia, I was in an accident that changed the course of my life for several months. I did not cause the accident; I was a victim of negligence. My arm was broken during the accident, and I had to undergo surgery. After surgery and the placement of screws in my arm, a couple days later, my arm became very painful and discolored. I called the doctor to share what was happening. They suggested going to the ER. After examination, it was determined that I had a major infection.

Because of the extent of the infection, I had to undergo surgery once again. They had to open my arm. While in the hospital, the infection became worse, and I was diagnosed with necrotizing fasciitis—an acute flesh-eating disease. The disease began to travel so fast up my arm that doctors told my wife if it traveled over my shoulder into the area of my heart, I could die that same day. They began to give me heavy antibiotics. The infection was so aggressive they had to move quickly. Meanwhile, Deloris and I watched my arm deteriorate.

The doctors were not satisfied with the antibiotics; therefore, I was transferred to another hospital for a few hours to undergo several bariatric treatments inside a long tube. I was placed inside whirlpools. My doctor was doing everything he could think of to save my arm. The entire ordeal was devastating.

My blood levels were crazy. One morning, the doctor came in and checked my levels and immediately took me back to surgery again. After surgery, he spoke to my wife and told her he had to give me a blood transfusion. He stated if he had not done so at that moment, he would've lost me on the operating table.

Deloris had the entire community, along with herself, praying for me. I remember her praying and reading to me scriptures that related to healing. She did not understand it at the time, but it was one of the greatest things she could have ever done to fortify my inner thought processing because during this whole process, I was heavily sedated which put me at a brain frequency called theta that, according to my studies, is just below consciousness.[29] This meant that my subconscious was receiving the information that it needed to work on as it related to my healing process. I remember so vividly reading some of the doctor's reports, saying that with the quantity of antibiotics they had given me, the infection should have died. My belief is that the positive reinforcement that was given to my mind along with the supernatural healing power of God is what sustained my body until the miracle of healing took place.

As time went on, I went into my fourth surgery. This was the greatest challenge of them all. The doctor told my wife that because of the progression of the infection, he might have to take my arm. He told her, "When I take him in the operating room, if I come back in fifteen minutes, I will need your permission to remove his arm." She told me that when she left the doctor, she went and prayed and felt like she touched heaven on my

29 Bruce Lipton, PhD, "Reprogram Your Subconscious Mind with These 3 Powerful Steps," *Fearless Soul*, 8 July 2019, https://iamfearlesssoul.com/reprogram-your-subconscious-mind-with-these-3-powerful-steps-bruce-lipton/.

behalf. Fifteen minutes went by, and the doctor did not come out. Twenty-five minutes went by, and the doctor didn't come out. After about an hour and a half, the doctor came out. He stated to my wife, "I don't know what happened, but there has been a turnaround. Things look better regarding his arm. It did not need to be removed."

The journey was not over. I underwent three more surgeries. Because 70 percent of the skin on my arm was gone from the infection, I had to undergo skin graft surgery. They had to take skin from my legs to use on my arm. Now, there was pain and more healing to take place in two areas of my body.

After two months, I was finally released from the hospital to heal from the skin graft surgery. My arm had about two hundred staples in it from surgery. Because of my poor health condition, when I returned home, I had to live in the downstairs area of my house on the sofa. I had no strength and no energy, and I was still on IV antibiotics at home. After about a week, I began to have pain in both of my legs. I could not walk. Things could not get any worse; but they did.

Blood clots in both legs took me back to the hospital. The doctors told me my possible path regarding the blood clots. Once again, they were very aggressive in trying to deal with this matter. I could not believe that I was back in the hospital again. After leaving, I was in a wheelchair for a few weeks. My healing process consisted of weekly travels to a specialist for infusions to continue to combat the disease. The healing was a long process. Three and a half months later, I was finally able, still healing, to sleep in my bed upstairs, in my house, for the first time.

Throughout the course of the entire process, and as grim as things got, I never believed I was going to lose my arm. I distinctly remember my pastor coming to visit with me. I could hear the concern in his voice as he said to me, "Do you understand what the doctors are saying?" My response was, "Yes, but I believe God!" The struggle between my emotions, my words, and my visualization was great. But my faith in the power of God and His ability to heal was greater.

THE STRUGGLE BETWEEN MY EMOTIONS, MY WORDS, AND MY VISUALIZATION WAS GREAT. BUT MY FAITH IN THE POWER OF GOD AND HIS ABILITY TO HEAL WAS GREATER.

I was in the hospital for over two months fighting for my life with this aggressive disease. I hope that this pushes you to a place of firm belief because believing has the power like no other to transform your life. My situation was my physical body, but your situation could be that you've been procrastinating. What if you—like me—just decided that nothing could shake your belief in your ability and the ability of God to partner with you to bring your dream to a reality? Let's look at the story of Markita Andrews. I read about it at the Scoutmaster's Minute website.[30]

Markita and her mother lived in New York. Markita's mother worked as a waitress after her husband left them. Markita was only eight years old, and her and her mother's dream was to travel the globe. One day, Markita's mother said to her, "I will work hard to make enough money to send you to college, and I know you'll go to college and graduate. Afterward, you will make enough money to take us around the world."

So at age thirteen, after reading in her Girl Scouts magazine that the Scout who sold the most cookies would win an all-expenses-paid trip for two around the world, Markita decided to sell all the Girl Scout cookies she could. Her goal was to sell more Girl Scout cookies than anyone else in the world. But desire alone was not enough to make her dream come true. Markita knew she needed a plan. She went to her aunt.

Her aunt advised:

Always wear the right outfit . . . your professional garb. When you are doing business, dress as if you are doing business. Wear your Girl Scout uniform, and be as professional as possible. When you go up to people in their tenement buildings at 4:30 or 6:30 pm and especially on Friday night, ask for a big order. Always smile, and

30 Jack Canfield and Mark V. Hansen, "Ask, Ask, Ask," *Scoutmasters Minute,* http://scoutmaster-minute.com/detail_ask-ask-ask.php.

*whether they buy or not, always be nice. Don't ask them
to buy your cookies; ask them to invest into your business.
Lots of other Scouts may want that trip around the world,
so you have to stand out amongst everyone.*

Lots of other Scouts had a plan, but only Markita went off in her uniform each day after her dream. Day after day Markita would leave her home and interact with different people. "Hi, I have a dream; I am earning a trip around the world for my mom and me by merchandising Girl Scout cookies," she would say at the door, "Would you like to invest in one dozen or two dozen boxes of cookies?"

Markita sold 3,526 boxes of Girl Scout cookies that year and won her trip around the world. Since then, she has sold more than forty-two thousand boxes. Markita Andrews stresses differentiating between short- and long-term goals, setting attainable goals, being polite and well-mannered, taking risks, using intuition, humor, and common sense, and accepting and dealing with fear and rejection.

She believed she could, so she did.

CHAPTER 9

WHAT MOVES YOU?

A ll of us have motivation of some sort; motivation is defined as the desire to achieve that which you would believe to be worthwhile. However, many people go through life never getting in touch with their greatness because of the lack of motivation to push themselves, and this is simply because they have not found something that they believe to be worthwhile to challenge them. You see, you must find a dream that will make you get up out of bed in the morning.

IN ORDER TO BE GREAT, YOU HAVE TO BE HUNGRY.

In order to be great, you have to be hungry. This is the single most important element that determines the quality of people's lives—not just the ability to have hunger but to be able to sustain it. Hunger means that you want more, more for yourself and more for others as well. You want to be the best expression of you that has ever been. Don't get satisfied with good. Jim Collins says, "Good is the enemy of GREAT,"[31] and most people start out with hunger at an early stage in life, but they lose it due to many reasons. What has taken away your ability to be hungry? Where did it stop? Where did you leave it? It's time to go back and pick it up.

Do this exercise. Take a moment to think, and go back to that place where you left your hunger or your drive. Now, pick it up in your hands. How does it feel? How does it look? Is it heavy or light? Listen quietly for sixty seconds. What do you hear? That dream is saying, *I still want to be a part of your life. I've been waiting for you, hoping that you would come back and get me so that we can work together again.*

One of the things we must do is we must be actively involved in achieving self-mastery. You must work on yourself continuously. Never be satisfied with average; always know that as you invest effort and time on you, you will be continuously evolving into the best version of you. That is the greatest ability that human beings have over animals. You see, a dog can't be anything but a dog. A tree can't be anything but a tree, but as a human being, you've got unlimited potential. You can put forth effort, and by concentrating on you and developing you, you can transform your life from wherever you are right now to wherever you desire to go.

---

31 Jim Collins, "Good Is the Enemy of Great," *Jim Collins—Video/Audio—Good Is the Enemy of Great*, 2017, https://www.jimcollins.com/media_topics/GoodIsTheEnemyOfGreat.html.

You've got to know and realize that you have greatness within you. You must begin to see a vision of yourself in the future, being and doing whatever it is that's inside of your heart. If just one person reading this book will capture the essence of what that means—that you have greatness in you and a responsibility to manifest that greatness—you will touch and transform millions of lives. The world will never be the same again because you came this way.

True champions get hungrier every time they win. Winners dominate losers, and legends dominate winners. A loser, a winner, or a legend—which are you? Now is the time. The talking is done, and you have to make a decision: Are you ready to take the next step?

In his book *Toward a Psychology of Being*, Abraham Maslow explains there are two powerful sets of forces within the human condition: a drive for growth and its opposing force, a drive for safety.[32] Growth propels us forward toward wholeness of self to discover our uniqueness. Its opposing force, safety, leads us to defend our current self, clinging to the familiar out of fear of the unknown. The force of safety keeps us where we are now—in the past and afraid to take chances that might improve our current conditions. Therefore, we are bound internally and externally. This safety-seeking side is afraid of independence, freedom, and separateness—the very things our growth side is demanding.

---

32 Abraham H. Maslow, *Toward a Psychology of Being* (Bensenville, IL: Lushena Books, 2014).

GROWTH PROPELS US FORWARD TOWARD WHOLENESS OF SELF TO DISCOVER OUR UNIQUENESS.

But I write to you in hopes that you are ready to tell safety and security goodbye. I believe what Scott Jeffrey says: "What we focus on tends to guide the direction of our lives. If we focus on the dangers of growth, our need for safety wins the day."[33] And that, if we minimize the dangers of our emerging uniqueness and fuller expression of self while enhancing our "attractions toward growth, a world of new possibilities presents itself."[34]

We are confronted daily with an ongoing series of choices between safety and growth, dependence or independence, regression or progression, immaturity or maturity. I pray that after reading this book, you are ready for a *Mindset . . . Reset.*

If you are ready, repeat this out loud:

"I can."
"I will."
"I must."

33 Scott Jeffrey, "Self Mastery: A Complete Guide to Actualizing Your Potential," *Scott Jeffrey*, 18 Feb. 2020, https://scottjeffrey.com/self-mastery/#:~:text=Self%20mastery%20is%20often%20defined,will%20to%20 realize%20that%20vision.
34 Scott Jeffrey, "Self Mastery: A Complete Guide to Actualizing Your Potential."

CHAPTER 10

REJECT REJECTION

Henry Wadsworth Longfellow wrote, "The heights by great men reached and kept were not attained by sudden flight, but they while their companions slept, were toiling upward in the night." He's saying that you have to work. You have to do your due diligence; you can't just sit around and hope something will happen.

ONE OF THE FEARS THAT STANDS BETWEEN YOU AND BEING SUCCESSFUL AND HAVING WHAT YOU WANT IS THE FEAR OF ASKING FOR WHAT YOU WANT.

The first action that you have to take is to simply ask. One of the fears that stands between you and being successful and having what you want is the fear of asking for what you want. Why don't people ask? They are afraid of rejection.

When a person feels a sense of being unwanted, that person is feeling rejection. David Dennison describes it this way:

You desire people to love you, yet you believe that they do not. You want to be a part of the group, but you feel excluded. Rejection occurs when love is withdrawn, knowingly or unknowingly, and the person is denied the right or opportunity to be accepted as they are. Rejection could be defined as the absence of meaningful love, and at its worst, a wanton disregard of another person and his or her needs.

Almost all of us have experienced rejection at one time or another, but many of us have not understood its nature or its effects. [Rejections are the most common emotional wounds we sustain in daily life.] It is obvious that such a universal syndrome as rejection would permeate all levels of society and its institutions. Since no one but God is capable of giving perfect love at all times and in every circumstance, some lack of love or imperfect love (rejection) will come into all of our lives.[35]

We all experience rejection differently. We all react to it differently. The way you respond to rejection is major as it relates to your future and desired destiny.

Rejection can damage our mood and self-esteem, it elicits swells of anger and aggression, and it destabilizes our need to belong. The fear of rejection can hold you back from taking risks and reaching

---

35 David Dennison, "Rectifying Rejection," *Sermon Central*, 5 Aug. 2013, https://www.sermoncentral.com/sermons/rectifying-rejection-dennis-davidson-sermon-on-rejection-177952.

for big goals. Thousands of individuals give up on their dreams and desired lives because of the fear of being rejected again.

The rejection you faced may have been something relatively minor—or it may have been so devastating that it affected your whole life and all of your relationships. Whether the rejection we experience is large or small, one thing that remains constant is the fact that it always hurts. Sometimes it hurts more than we expect. Just as hurt people hurt people, rejected people reject people and ultimately, they reject God. In many instances, they do it subconsciously. People that have experienced major rejections in their lives are often insecure in their relationships with people and with God. Sometimes, we wonder why people follow the crowd or seem to fall for anything. It's because rejected people are susceptible to peer pressure. They will go along with the crowd to feel wanted.

WHETHER THE REJECTION WE EXPERIENCE IS LARGE OR SMALL, ONE THING THAT REMAINS CONSTANT IS THE FACT THAT IT ALWAYS HURTS.

Rejection gives birth to self-centeredness. This is when a person becomes independent of outside force or influence. They become solely concerned with their own desires and needs. They want to care for others, but their subconscious mind will not allow them to. I know, on numerous occasions, you have tried to figure out a person's negative behavior towards moving forward and even your own negative behavior; perhaps rejection is holding you all captive. Your paralytic state originates in your subconscious mind. Because this is an unfortunate part of life every individual will encounter, we have to learn how to RESET our minds, so it does not affect our lives forever.

Dennison goes to on to say, "Rejection occurring early in childhood and the severity of that rejection are usually determining factors in the amount of damage sustained by the rejected personality."[36] Thousands of adults today are still operating in childhood rejection. Is that you? Many individuals remain stuck—stagnated and frustrated—and fear moving forward with their dreams because the rejection becomes rooted in their subconscious. However, there are those who have been rejected and used that rejection to persevere in life and make their dreams become a reality.

Dennison lists many reasons people feel rejected:

You were not chosen to play on a school sports team; your first boyfriend failed to show up for an important date and never gave you a reason; you were not accepted at the college of your choice; you were laid off from your job for no good reason.

Far worse than these examples is the pain that comes because you never felt love from your father, you sensed

---

36 David Dennison, "Rectifying Rejection."

*your mother didn't want you, you experienced an angry
divorce; you were the unfavored child, were abused, had
some handicap, or some public humiliation.*[37]

Rejection also takes place when acceptance is contingent upon
satisfactory performance. If you don't measure up to someone's or
some group's imaginary standards, you are rejected. And the list
goes on. Experiences such as these can leave permanent wounds,
whether you are aware of them or not. You can be healed from the
wounds that come from rejection. If you learn to accept yourself,
you will be able to adequately show love to others. But before you
can receive help, you must recognize the nature of your problem.
You must acknowledge and accept responsibility and move forward. Yes, God can help you, but you have to partner with Him
to obtain complete victory.

YES, YOU CAN GET OUT OF REJECTION'S DEATH GRIP!

The first step to overcoming rejection is to recognize the problem.
Once you recognize it, you can deal with it. Yes, you can get out
of rejection's death grip! You could be one phone call away from
your YES. You could be one footstep away from achieving a major
goal. Will you RESET and determine to live your best life? You
have a choice to make. Learn to forgive and accept forgiveness. I
encourage you to make the right choice and live.

37 David Dennison, "Rectifying Rejection."

Charles Solomon wrote in *The Rejection Syndrome*:

> *Those who have been rejected are prone to pass along some form of rejection to those closest to them. Until those who have been rejected find the life-transforming love of Christ as the only complete antidote to rejection-based symptoms, they turn to pursuits which they hope, consciously or unconsciously, will make them acceptable to themselves and others.*[38]

To conquer rejection, you must not allow the external to determine your internal. You may be saying subconsciously, *So many bad things have happened in my life that I expect bad things rather than good.* Your vibrational frequency is set at being rejected because you have not elevated your thoughts to a higher vibrational frequency that assures you that God has better for you. It doesn't matter who doesn't love you because your Father—God—loves you. You have to change your mindset from that of defeat to one of victory and conquest, declaring, *I will no longer be held captive by my past. Therefore, in Jesus' name, I have favor with God, and I have favor with man, and I expect nothing but success.*

IT DOESN'T MATTER WHO DOESN'T LOVE YOU BECAUSE YOUR FATHER—GOD—LOVES YOU.

---

38 Charles R. Solomon, *The Rejection Syndrome* (Wheaton, IL: Tyndale House, 1984) 12.

When you expect to be rejected, that's what you create for your world. You will always be rejected because that's what you expect. Your mind, your words, your thoughts, and your emotions are all programmed for rejection. You must reprogram your mind and not allow externals to determine your internals. We all have work to do when it comes to changing our thinking. Being in charge of your thoughts is some of the hardest work you'll ever do in your life. And it can't be just one hour a day that you focus on it; you must do this all day long—every day—until mastering it just becomes who you are. You have to start seeing that you can have control over this by changing your thinking. Change what you speak out of your mouth. If you keep at it, one day, you will get to a place where you don't have to work at it. It's just who you are.

CHAPTER 11

PULL THE TRIGGER

During this study, there have been many "aha" moments. Two of the biggest have been that we have the ability to create the world that we desire to live in, and we can shape that world positively or negatively. During this writing process, I remembered when I was a child. Growing up, we would say to one another—once we got very angry, with tears in our eyes, perhaps huffing and puffing—"You make me sick!" The reality is that taking on that mindset as a child and never going through the process of dealing with and getting relief from the pain of those emotions really could make someone sick!

A child who carries that emotion into their adolescent stage, where it intensifies, could turn into a teen that acts out on it by becoming physical with their peers. Whenever there is a moment of anger, if it has never been properly dealt with, it intensifies when we're older. We become hardwired for extreme emotions. By adulthood, it has become a stronghold deeply embedded within our subconscious mind.

Have you ever seen someone who was enraged, but they couldn't really tell you the reason why? It could be the result of an unhealed hurt that was never dealt with. As a result of internalizing what they have experienced, they literally make themselves sick because their perception stirs the emotions that produce the negative chemicals in the body. We always have a choice of how we respond to situations and circumstances and the way they will affect us. If we give too much significance to externals, we allow our externals to affect our internals. We cannot afford to allow people and circumstances to determine what emotions we're going to feel, what thoughts we are going to have, or what actions we're going to take. When we do that, we allow our Christ-consciousness to decrease.

IF WE GIVE TOO MUCH SIGNIFICANCE TO EXTERNALS, WE ALLOW OUR EXTERNALS TO AFFECT OUR INTERNALS.

Initially, we must make a conscious decision to stop giving significance to things that don't have any real consequence in the long run. We must realize that it is not in our best interest to continue down that path and make a commitment to do the work of mastering ourselves. You have to intentionally tell your mind, *The world is not doing this to me! I am going to be in control of my thoughts and emotions because they create my reality.*

Dr. James Richards, in his book *How To Stop the Pain*, writes that if we would stop giving so much significance to people and things, we would stop criticizing and judging. Then, we would not have all of the emotional pain.[39] We only have pain according to the level of significance we give something. If you practice these principles you can become free of the anxiety from worrying about what people think. It is all about taking control of your emotions, and the only way to do that is to take control of your thoughts.

If you set an intention and purpose that you're not going to give these things any significance, then, when you catch yourself doing it ask yourself, *What is it in me that is causing me to give this person (or circumstance) so much significance?* Understand that there are people in the world with souls badly damaged from unmet needs, unhealed hurts, and unresolved issues. The things they are dealing with—that you take on—have nothing to do with you! You just may be a trigger for the things that are in their souls.

Triggers are situations, places, words, people, or even smells that remind you of past pain or trauma. They can send you into a place of despair, anger, or anxiety. We see triggers as an event or circumstance that causes either an emotional or behavioral response. They are reminders that push us into some type of destructive thought which causes us to respond in a negative way. The reminder is usually associated with previous failures, past hurts, disappointments, or broken relationships. The issue lasts longer than it should because we don't know how to stop the destructive thought or behavior.

---

39 James B. Richards, *How to Stop the Pain* (New Kensington, PA: Whitaker House, 2001).

When we call something a trigger, we shift our emotional control from our heart to the person, place, or situation that previously hurt us because we have connected the issue with an emotion. We mistakenly think the trigger is the cause, but we have developed habits of thoughts in response to the pain that leads to the predictable emotional condition.

Undoubtedly, you've thought to yourself, *If this goes against what the Father wants and desires for us, why does He let it happen?* Why is there a chasm between what God wants and what we experience? Could it be that there is something that is inhibiting our ability to experience life as God has intended? Perhaps we are facing an emotional epidemic of triggers. Can I suggest to you that triggers are contributing to many people languishing?

WHY IS THERE A CHASM BETWEEN WHAT GOD WANTS AND WHAT WE EXPERIENCE? COULD IT BE THAT THERE IS SOMETHING THAT IS INHIBITING OUR ABILITY TO EXPERIENCE LIFE AS GOD HAS INTENDED?

Consider this: A couple retired, moved to Georgia, and joined a local assembly. The wife was always an exceptional leader and did not require a high level of oversight. As a result of knowing this, the pastor didn't feel the need to be hands-on or to micromanage this individual. She was proficient when it came to her ability to maneuver and interact with people; therefore, not much attention was given to her. She noticed, internalized that to mean she was being rejected, and decided to make an appointment to meet with the pastor to discuss why she felt that way.

She learned that she did not get a lot of attention in terms of doing the work because the pastor knew that she was well able to stand on her own. This was a high compliment to her. However, because she'd had some bad experiences with the pastor's wife at the church she came from, she transferred those bad experiences onto the new pastor. The fact that Brenda didn't get the attention she desired triggered her to feel as if she were being rejected.

Our response of despair, depression, anxiety and/or anger reveals that we are ignoring God and disregarding His promises regarding healing from the brokenness in and around us. Instead of thinking in terms of triggers, we need to see certain situations and people as clues, signals, or reminders to change our thoughts to be more God-oriented. This would lead us to a place of repentance and a deeper trust in God and His word.

Another example involves Professor McAfee. The professor was confused and didn't know why she needed to forgive her student Bill; to her knowledge, he had not done anything wrong to her. Through a conversation, Bill revealed to her that when he was in her class, he disliked her. He'd had to pray to God for help so that he wouldn't dislike her so much, especially because he really didn't know why he disliked her. Bill admitted that Professor McAfee hadn't done anything to him!

After thinking about it and asking himself the question, *What is it in me that is causing me to give this person (or circumstance) so much significance?* he finally realized he had transferred the emotions he felt for his drill sergeant to Professor McAfee. Like his drill sergeant, she was Caucasian and about the same size. They both had the same color eyes and hair. Bill had had some bad experiences with his drill sergeant, and he had taken those bad experiences, buried deep in his subconscious, and transferred them to Professor McAfee. She also had requirements: Bill had to do his work, and he had to come to class regularly. So all of the things that were embedded in his subconscious mind that he didn't like about his drill sergeant he transferred onto the professor. Having Professor McAfee as an instructor triggered all of his bad feelings about his drill sergeant. To conquer this, Bill needed a reset.

What we must do as individuals is make sure that we expand our understanding of God's deliverance. We tend to think that deliverance can only come in one way, and the preferred, most desired, or favored way is by divine intervention. While I believe in divine intervention, the vast majority of the deliverance that we can receive assuredly will come from knowledge. And when we look at this, I am not only speaking of spiritual knowledge. God wants us to be educated with life principles that will free us from the bondage of our souls.

WE TEND TO THINK THAT DELIVERANCE CAN ONLY COME IN ONE WAY.

God has richly endowed the earth realm with an enormous amount of data. It is said that this is the age of information, but I encourage you to not just get the information. Instead, begin to make implementation. The Word of God clearly tells us in Hosea 4:6 (KJV), "My people are destroyed for lack of knowledge: because thou hast rejected knowledge, I will also reject thee." As a believer, I would not want it to be my lot that the hand of God is tied on my behalf due to the fact that deliverance came to me in the form of knowledge, but I wanted it in the divine intervention. Therefore, I rejected it which leaves me stuck in my present condition. If this is you, it's time for a reset.

Theologian John Calvin referred to it as the mortification of the flesh—the putting to death of the appetite and urges that we have as imperfect beings that have a tendency to push us to engage in self-sabotaging behavior that not only destroys our life, but it destroys other people's lives as well. That thing does not go to death by itself. It must be put to death . . . *daily*.

The apostle Paul put it this way in 1 Corinthians 15:31 (KJV): "I die daily." I can imagine him continuing ". . . and every day, I make a decision to bury the old me." In Romans 7 (author paraphrase), he says:

I see two natures on the inside of me. . . . One part of me wants to do what God wants, and the other part of me wants to do what I want. . . . The evil that I would not do is what I find myself doing, and the good that I want to do is what I find myself not doing. So I realize that when I do what I don't want to do—even though I really want to do it—it's not me that's doing it. It's sin that lives within me. . . . Who shall deliver me from this wretched body of death?

Yes, some people experience that supernatural intervention against an appetite, but for some people, the roots are deep, and they have been there for so long. Without miraculous supernatural intervention, deliverance is going to look a lot like self-control.

Have you ever said, "Lord, I thought I had conquered that!" and all of a sudden, there it is again—you're triggered? If the answer is yes, and if you are going to overcome it, you will have to learn how to get to the root of the trigger. Things like insecurity will trap you. You may still be ensnared by self-doubt because you haven't learned how to reset and eradicate the thing that triggers it!

It is time for us to get rid of that flawed theology that says deliverance will come to everybody in the same way every time. I would like to suggest to you that just as your calling is customized, your liberation and your freedom and your flourishing are customized, too.

JUST AS YOUR CALLING IS CUSTOMIZED, YOUR LIBERATION AND YOUR FREEDOM AND YOUR FLOURISHING ARE CUSTOMIZED, TOO.

The things that trigger us can take many different forms; some are obvious while others are more subtle. It comes natural for us to deny, excuse, blame, or suppress our triggers by distracting ourselves through some form of "self-medication." An intentional and crucial skill we need to develop is the ability to identify when we are triggered, take ownership for what we feel, and be willing to admit it. For some of us, it is much easier to say:

» "I'm having a bad day." (Blame the circumstance.)

» "He makes me so mad." (Blame someone else.)

» "I'm just not myself today." (I'm not sure who is being blamed here.)

OUR EMOTIONAL STATUS IS A DEAD GIVEAWAY OF BEING TRIGGERED.

The primary way we know when we are triggered is by what we are feeling in the moment. If we are feeling something other than peace, something is wrong. Our emotional status is a dead giveaway of being triggered. Our emotions are activated by how we interpret moments. No matter what is going on around us, it is not the situation that is producing what we feel.

This is a hard principle for many people to embrace. One reason for this difficulty is we somehow think that if we do not blame the person or the situation for our emotions, then we are minimizing what was done in the situation itself. This is not so. What happened may very well be unjust, inappropriate, or downright evil. Nevertheless, we feel whatever we believe and not because of what has happened.

Our outward behavior can be an indication of our being triggered. Some of our behaviors are so spontaneous and habitual that we do not even notice the pain behind them. For example, overeating, compulsive buying, biting our nails, undue concern about our appearance, obsessive religious rituals, and even much of the good things we may do in our Christian service, can be examples of this. However, if we are willing to slow things down and examine what we are doing and why we are doing it, we may discover that some of our behavior is a symptom of the lies we believe being triggered.

A simple question we can ask ourselves is, *Why am I doing what I am doing?* We should probably throw out the first thing that comes to our minds in that it is most likely not the truth. We are prone to lie to ourselves about why we do what we do and to over-spiritualize our actions, blame others, or make excuses. Asking ourselves this question is designed to get to the heart of, or motive for, why we are doing what we are doing.

There is a good chance we will find that our behavior is a catharsis to the emotions we do not want to feel. The only people who do not experience some measure of emotional pain from time to time are those who have so suppressed what they feel that they have become consciously unaware of it. No one has perfect truth-based thinking; we are all infected with lies. Since we will feel whatever we believe, our lies will eventually be triggered, and we will feel whatever the lie produces. There are no exceptions.

NO ONE HAS PERFECT TRUTH-BASED THINKING; WE ARE ALL INFECTED WITH LIES. SINCE WE WILL FEEL WHATEVER WE BELIEVE, OUR LIES WILL EVENTUALLY BE TRIGGERED, AND WE WILL FEEL WHATEVER THE LIE PRODUCES. THERE ARE NO EXCEPTIONS.

The good news is, however, that emotional pain is our friend. It provides us with a warning, pointing out our lie-based thinking and providing continual opportunities for us to have our minds renewed. As we choose to take ownership for what we feel and look to the Lord for the truth, we can cooperate with God as He refines our faith, renews our minds, and transforms our lives.

Neuroscientist Dr. Joe Dispenza defines a habit as "a redundant set of automatic, unconscious thoughts, behaviors and emotions that's been acquired through repetition."[40] A habit is when you have done something so many times that your body now knows how to do it better than your mind. The only way to break this cycle is a RESET, and it has to be deliberate, intentional, strategic, and clearly defined. Otherwise, you will not be able to defeat this stronghold.

For instance, you wake up in the morning, and you begin to think about your problems. Your problems are circuits or memories in the brain. Each one of those memories is connected to people and things from certain times and places. Therefore, your brain is a record of the past. That means that the very moment you start your day, you're already thinking in the past, and if you stay with that train of thought, you'll continue to relive and recreate the thoughts, the visualization, and the emotions of your past.

Or, let's say a woman finds out after being in a marriage for five years that her husband has gone outside of their covenant and fathered children. She divorces him and does not seek out the proper counsel to get over the hurt and guilt of feeling like she failed him in some way. So she ends up waking up every morning thinking, *What if I had done something differently? Maybe this*

40 Joe Dispenza, "A Habit," *Life Connection Church Kuwait*, Apr. 2019, https://lifeconnectionchurchkw.com/wp-content/uploads/2019/04/A-Habit-Joe-Dispenza.pdf.

wouldn't have happened. Her thoughts then become something like, *I will never trust another man because all men are the same!* Her visualization becomes that of seeing herself in another relationship and going through the same thing. Her emotions become repeatedly the same emotions that she felt when this happened to her years ago: sorrow, low self-esteem, worthlessness—and her desire to better herself physically or socially is almost nonexistent. She continuously blames herself, failing to realize that she's not responsible for her partner's actions.

To conquer such a thing, I feel that it is of the utmost importance that we are able to process this through the lenses of both the scientific reason—the chemical reason—we feel the way that we do as well as the theological fortification that we can find and receive from the Word of God and from having a real relationship with our Creator. There was a time when science and theology were one discipline. That thought is not strange to me because when you take the time to study them both, you see that they go hand in hand.

For instance, the Bible says in Proverbs 23:7 (NKJV), "As [a man] thinks in his heart, so *is* he." And as of late, scientists have discovered that there are forty thousand cells in your heart that are not heart cells—they are brain cells.[41] So God, at the beginning, by design, created us in a way that—at times—we would think from our heart. In this, we see the two working together to give clarity and insight as to how science and theology work together.

41 Ali M. Alshami, "Pain: Is It All in the Brain or the Heart?" *Current Pain and Headache Reports*, US National Library of Medicine, 14 Nov. 2019, https://pubmed.ncbi.nlm.nih.gov/31728781/#:~:text=Recent%20findings%3A%20Dr.,has%20its%20own%20nervous%20system.

James 1:9 (KJV) states, "A double minded man is unstable in all his ways." And the apostle Paul, in 2 Corinthians 10:5 (NIV), taught, "We demolish arguments and every pretension that sets itself up against the knowledge of God, and we take captive every thought to make it obedient to Christ." Taking every thought captive sounds simple, but it isn't easy. It takes a tremendous amount of dedication and self-awareness. It requires repentance from sin and faith in God, but it will be the most rewarding gift you could ever give yourself. Perhaps you struggle with anxiety in your thought life. You can form a plan for taking every thought captive.

"Life and death are in the power of the tongue," according to Proverbs 18:21 (KJV). How you think determines your words, and your words determine your world. Therefore, it is vitally important that we do the work within our minds so that when we open our mouths to speak, we are speaking things that are in line with our visions for our lives. One should take care to watch his or her words, understanding the power of speech. Perhaps you know the phrase, "You will be eating your words." If you love to talk, you will eat the fruit of your words.

We hear all the time that we must guard our gates. This is true. Guarding your gates is crucial because your gates are the entryway into your subconscious. Whatever you give your attention to is then drawn to you, and that's what you become.

CHAPTER 12

FINE FOCUS

t is said that where focus goes, energy flows. We must be ever consciously mindful of what we focus on. If we're not, we will be fully led and governed by our subconscious minds. And this, sadly, is what we see perpetuated throughout the world today. A vast majority of people are controlled by their subconscious minds; thus, we get the current condition of society.

WE MUST BE EVER CONSCIOUSLY MINDFUL OF WHAT WE FOCUS ON.

One might ask the question, "How is it that a mother could carry a child for nine months, give birth to it, and walk off and leave the child to either die or be raised by a complete stranger?" That could happen for any number of reasons, but it's possible the mother's soul had so many unhealed hurts, unmet needs, and unresolved issues due to her first seven years of scripting and modeling that she never bonded with the child in pregnancy or afterwards. Again, this goes back to the internal downloads that we receive in our formative years. Perhaps *her* mother never bonded with her, so the model she received left her with feelings of abandonment which make it difficult for any woman to connect with her child. Thus—the need for a reset.

By force of habit, we wake up in the morning, sit on the side of the bed, scroll through our social media, and check emails. As a result, we feel really connected to life. This becomes like a program, and we lose our free will to it. Then, when it comes to changing the redundancy, it's challenging because, within our subconscious mind, we have created a system that drives us to act in a way that is against our best interests yet we feel compelled to follow it.

Dr. Dispenza says that 95 percent of who we are by age thirty-five is a set of memorized behaviors and emotional reactions.[42] Beliefs and perceptions act like a computer that has been programmed. So a person can say, "I am going to change my lifestyle and my eating habits," and sincerely want to be free. However, the mind has been previously hardwired to think another way and do something totally different than this new thought, so there is a great level of resistance presenting a great struggle between the body and the mind.

We see people in this position every day and not only as it relates to what they eat. It relates to people that are in abusive relationships—whether physical or verbal—that stay in these relationships because they have become accustomed to the cycle. Rather than

---

42 "Don't Wait for Tragedy, You Can Also Change Your Life in a State of Joy and Inspiration," *The Indian Express*, 8 Apr. 2020, https://indianexpress.com/article/lifestyle/life-positive/dont-wait-for-tragedy-you-can-also-change-your-life-in-a-state-of-joy-and-inspiration-6351854/.

break outside of the cycle and change, they stay with the familiar, and days become weeks, weeks become months, and months become years. As a result of their environment and their emotional state, signs and symptoms of their unhappiness begin to show up in their bodies in the form of sickness and disease.

To begin to make those changes, Dr. Dispenza says you must "access the analytical mind because what separates the conscious mind from the subconscious mind is the analytical mind"[43] which involves the use of logical reasoning. The only way to change the hardwiring of your brain is by reprogramming the subconscious so that you're producing different kinds of thoughts since it's your thoughts producing that chemical release that causes your brain to get hardwired a certain way.

ONE OF THE MAJOR WAYS TO RE-HARDWIRE YOUR BRAIN IS BY FOCUSING THROUGH MEDITATION.

One of the major ways to re-hardwire your brain is by focusing through meditation. I came to grips with this concept a few years ago. Deloris was away studying and preparing feverishly for a presentation that was to take place in a few days. She was in her native state of South Carolina, and her mother began to see the

43 "Joe Dispenza on How to Reprogram Your Subconscious Mind," *Fearless Motivation,* 7 Nov. 2019, https://www.fearlessmotivation.com/2019/11/07/joe-dispenza-on-how-to-reprogram-your-subconscious-mind/.

anxiety caused by prolonged intense studying. Her mother simply told her, "Step away from your studies, and begin to meditate." Much to my wife's surprise, it worked! That was one of the most profoundly delivered presentations that she had ever given. And meditation, of course, changed her approach to preparing for future presentations as well as her outlook on life moving forward. This was indeed a Mindset–RESET.

According to the website The Medguru:

> *Meditation is a mental exercise that involves relaxation, focus, and self-awareness. Meditation is to the mind what physical exercise is to the body. The practice is usually done individually, in a still, seated position, and with eyes closed.*[44]

I would like for us to focus our attention on relaxation. I believe that this is one of the greatest challenges facing our generation. We have become so driven, career-focused, impatient, anxious, and narcissistic that we have lost our ability to just relax.

It is a proven point that in order to change your state of mind, you must change your physiology, and most of the time, in order to do this, you must change your surroundings. Changing your surroundings usually means you will have to "unplug" in order to become relaxed enough to meditate. In our immediate world, any number of things surround us, seeking to distract us and keep

---

44 Khushi, "What Is Meditation?" *The Med Guru*, 29 Sept. 2021, https://themedguru.com/2021/09/what-is-meditation/.html.

us from relaxation. Relaxation is important because it helps to release a chemical in our bodies that promotes healing of the mind, body, and ultimately, the soul. Let's look first at the importance and benefits of relaxation.

Got Questions Ministries provides a comprehensive biblical understanding:

> *"Rest" is defined as "peace, ease or refreshment." "Relax" means "to become loose or less firm, to have a milder manner, to be less stiff." The Bible speaks quite highly of rest. It is a repeated theme throughout Scripture, beginning with the creation week* (Genesis 2:2-3). *God created for six days; then He rested, not because He was tired but to set the standard for mankind to follow. The Ten Commandments made resting on the Sabbath a requirement of the Law* (Exodus 20:8-11). *Notice that God said, "Remember the Sabbath." It wasn't something new; it had been around since creation. All God's people and their servants and the animals were to have one day in seven to rest. The command to rest was not an excuse to be lazy. You had to work for six days to get to the Sabbath. The land also needed to rest* (Leviticus 25:4, 8-12). *God is very serious about rest. God desires rest for us because it does not come naturally to us. To rest, we have to trust that God will take care of things for us. We have to trust that, if we take a day off, the world will not stop turning on its axis. From the beginning* (Genesis 3), *when we decided that we would start making*

all the decisions, mankind has become more tense and less able to relax. It was disobedience in the Garden that started the problem, but obedience now will bring the rest that God so desires for us (Hebrews 3:7 - 4:11). If one of the definitions of "relax" is "to become less firm," then relaxing our grip on our own lives, careers, families, etc., and giving them over to God in faith is the best way to relax. For the Christian, the ultimate rest is found in Christ. He invites all who are "weary and burdened" to come to Him and cast our cares on Him (Matthew 11:28; 1 Peter 5:7). It is only in Him that we find our complete rest—from the cares of the world, from the sorrows that plague us, and from the need to work to make ourselves acceptable to Him.

We can now cease our spiritual labors and rest in Christ, not just one day a week, but always.

WE CAN NOW CEASE OUR SPIRITUAL LABORS AND REST IN CHRIST, NOT JUST ONE DAY A WEEK, BUT ALWAYS.

Resting releases four main brain chemicals: dopamine, serotonin, oxytocin, and endorphins. They are often known as happy chemicals. Together, they play a role in how you experience happiness.

» **Dopamine** is a neurotransmitter produced by the hypothalamus, a small region of the brain that helps you feel pleasure.

» **Serotonin** is a chemical that carries messages between nerve cells in the brain and throughout your body. Serotonin plays a key role in such body functions as mood, sleep, digestion, nausea, wound healing, bone health, blood clotting, and sexual desire.[45]

» **Oxytocin** is typically linked to warm, fuzzy feelings and shown in some research to lower stress and anxiety. Oxytocin has the power to regulate our emotional responses and pro-social behaviors, including trust, empathy, gazing, positive memories, processing of bonding cues, and positive communication.[46]

» **Endorphins** are chemicals (hormones) your body releases when it feels pain or stress. They're released during pleasurable activities such as exercise, massage, eating, and sex. Endorphins help relieve pain, reduce stress, and improve your sense of well-being.[47]

There are dozens of meditational benefits recorded in scientifically proven studies that will keep you healthy, help prevent multiple diseases, make you emotionally well, and improve your performance.

---

45 "Serotonin: What Is It, Function & Levels," *Cleveland Clinic*, https://my.clevelandclinic.org/health/articles/22572-serotonin.
46 Sean Lewis, "The Global Dog Art Gallery Creates Connections with Pet Photography as Image Therapy," *SLR Lounge*, 31 Aug. 2021, https://www.slrlounge.com/the-global-dog-art-gallery-creates-connections-with-pet-photography-as-image-therapy/.
47 "Endorphins: What They Are and How to Boost Them," Cleveland Clinic, https://my.clevelandclinic.org/health/body/23040-endorphins.

I would like for us to explore two types of reset: a surface reset and a hard reset. We tend, as individuals, to lean more towards a surface reset. We reset our faces and our facial expressions so that people can't see the true feelings that we are experiencing. We have become masterful at masking what we feel, and we do that for so many reasons. We take what we feel, and we tuck it away neatly, thinking that if we don't deal with it, it will just go away. This is a terrible misnomer because it only leads to greater emotional damage.

I was consulting with a client the other day, and he was wondering why he would feel guilty when he would decline the opportunity to do business with very outspoken individuals. After consulting for a while, we discovered that there was a deep-rooted reason for him not wanting to embrace a person with a very direct personality. It was because it would remind him of his relationship with his father who was very abrasive and condescending.

As I began to discuss this, my client began to become tearful, and we paused to discuss why he was shedding the tears. The tears were a result of the pain that was surfacing because of his relationship with his father. As we began to further process his emotions, we discovered that he had simply decided to suppress his feelings and move on with life thus only giving him a surface reset.

We must understand that when we take this approach we are not doing the work of self-mastery. Therefore, we are allowing our brains to create a hardwire of emotional trauma that will inevitably control our future.

So we first had to deal with the question of if he were willing to go through the process to receive inner healing. No change can ever take place in our lives if we are not willing to own the fact that there is an issue and commit to doing the work of getting to the root of the issue. This speaks to the concept of cause and effect. His previous relationship with his father was the cause. The outward manifestation of his actions was the effect that had been created.

The process is never easy because the process calls us to look deep within at some things that we have compartmentalized and put in a place where we do not have to confront them. Many times, the pain or trauma has been placed so deeply that we have forgotten that it even exists. But in order to have a hard reset, we must confront the programs that have been previously hardwired in our subconscious. We cannot put our new information on top of an old program and expect to get new results. The minute you put it in, it becomes polluted with everything that's already there.

For the sake of imagery, if I take a bowl of clear water, and I put red coloring in it, immediately, it changes from clear to red. However, if I add another color, it becomes a combination of the two colors, and if I then add another color once again, it changes to a mixture of the three colors. It's neither the original color that I intended for it to be from the beginning nor will it ever be clear again. My original intent was to create something new, bright, and radiant, but by adding additional colors, it only became darker and less appealing. The only way to create something new with this design is to pour the water out and start again with clear water.

I hope this helps you see that in order to get a clear defined reset in your mind, you have to delete some things—painful, hurtful bitter things—but once you commit to the process, you start a journey to having your desired life. In our example, throwing the water out constitutes a hard reset. This is the only solution to changing the programming that we have obtained over the years that has created the self-sabotaging habits and limiting belief systems that we encounter on a daily basis.

The greatest challenge for my client was getting him to start the process. Even though he acknowledged a desire to start, it took a few sessions to get him to actually start. Many times, it is difficult to start because starting means that you must commit to facing the pain once again. His relationship with his father dealt with a lot of mental abuse, which consequently led to feelings of not being worthy to be loved, valued, or appreciated. Therefore, anytime someone would begin to show these emotions towards him, he would shut down immediately. He felt unworthy of them.

These things became barriers to anything or anyone getting close enough to love him. He became estranged to his family and friends. They all made numerous attempts to rescue him but all to no avail. He had become isolated, and his excuse was that he was inundated with work. However, we must understand that becoming inundated with work will never take the place of love and fulfillment because we were created with a need to be loved and fulfilled. So no matter how much we try to fill that space with other things, we will always have a void until we deal with the unmet needs, unhealed hurts, or unresolved issues.

CHAPTER 13

PERCEIVING IS BELIEVING

A s individuals, we often fail to acknowledge or even attempt to understand the scientific aspect of why we do what we do. In many instances, I believe that if we could learn to understand scientifically why we do what we do, it would empower us to intelligently pursue a course that would enable us to eradicate strongholds in our self-help strategies, thus alleviating a lot of the self-sabotaging habits that we have adopted in our lifestyles. The obstacles that come about as a result of the hardwiring in our subconscious mind are real. They pose an extremely difficult challenge to having healthy relationships and living fruitful lives.

THE OBSTACLES THAT COME ABOUT AS A RESULT OF THE HARDWIRING IN OUR SUBCONSCIOUS MIND ARE REAL.

I was speaking with a middle-aged man whose father was absent from his life. He felt as if he had spent the majority of his life searching for something—literally fighting for it—and his comment was, "The struggle is real." He was right! The challenge of learning to *be* a father when you did not have an active father in your life leaves you searching for a model to pattern your life after.

Meanwhile, throughout the process, you make mistakes, damaging relationships, drowning in your own insecurities, and making the lives of those who try to love you absolutely miserable. Questioning the validity and sincerity of any and every person who says that they love you pushes you to a lonely and isolated place. If there is not a RESET of the mindset, the individual has the potential of self-sabotaging good relationships and destroying the potential for future relationships.

In January 2011, Deloris and I launched a full-time ministry in the metro Atlanta area. In 2018, the board of the ministry that owned the building presented to my staff and me their current situation. They had a balloon payment due, and they could not afford it. However, they said to me, "If your ministry desires to have this building and can come up with more than $700,000, we will not put the building on the market." My thought was, *Is this really happening?* Prior to this meeting, there were many, many days I went to the building, put my key in the door, and pondered whether or not—someday—it could be ours.

When I found out the amount of money that was owed on the building, my first thought was, *This is a major undertaking.* My second thought was, *Is this the fulfillment of the promise?* I proceeded to examine all of the church accounts, and we only had $10,000 total in the bank. Also, we did not have enough giving units to qualify for a loan. I was encouraged by my mentor to make an offer of $500,000—an offer with nothing in the bank to back it up. If I had still been operating in my financial knowledge the way I was raised, I would have sabotaged the future of my destiny. My answer would have been absolutely no. I thank God for the knowledge that RESET MY MIND to see finance through another set of lenses.

With encouragement, I decided to step out on faith. I had nothing to lose. We made the $500,000 offer, and it was immediately rejected by the bank. One of the pastors of the church we were renting from spoke with the bank officials on our behalf, and this helped the bank see our offer from another perspective. Within the hour, the bank agreed to take the $500,000 offer with special stipulations that we had to close within thirty days. However, there still was no money. The Lord spoke to me very clearly and told me to give Him twelve hours of prayer. In obedience, I called forth a prayer meeting. Several members came throughout the day, and we prayed for twelve hours. We are so thankful for all of the parishioners who stood with us.

We previously discussed in this book the importance of prayer and meditation: As a result of prayer, meditation, and persistence, within seven days, my mentor and I were able to pull together three investors who brought $500,000 to the table, and we were on our way to closing. We became owners of the building in May 2018, and we went into ownership with immediate equity. Today the building is valued at over $1.5 million. My sincere belief is that if I had not had a reset in my thought process as it relates to money, I would not have been able to walk into this great blessing. When you embrace the concept of self-mastery, it carries over into every area of your life.

A person's perception is their particular attitude toward or way of regarding something. It has been said, "We see things not as they are, but as *we* are." Wise teachers have embraced that adage over the last several centuries because it is so true. We tend to see the world through the lenses of our own experiences, which can be positive or negative. It is these experiences that help to shape our worldview. For instance, a person grows up in an environment with both parents in the home working together in harmony to advance their lives and receiving positive results. As a result of seeing this example, this individual may have a proclivity to lean more in the direction of following the same life pattern.

WE TEND TO SEE THE WORLD THROUGH THE LENSES OF OUR OWN EXPERIENCES.

On the other hand, an individual grows up in a home with one parent who works very hard and is never home because they want to make sure that every need in the home is met. Subsequently, this individual could grow up with a great sense of independence that causes them to shun a partnership where two people work closely together. It could affect that person's ability to connect with others and work together in a corporate setting.

We think that we see the world as it is, but the truth is that we see the world as we are. Our external conditions will always affect our internal thought process. Who we are—our being—forms a paradigm through which we see the world.

So then, it is important to be aware of the things that influence our perception. We know that our paradigms determine how we see life; how we see, in turn, determines how we act and what we emulate. What we emulate (our actions) determines the results we get. To change the results we are getting, we need to start by changing our paradigm or our perception. This requires that we become consciously aware of our own biases and the things that impact our perception of the world and the people we encounter on a daily basis.

The impact of doing this is evident in Teddy's story as told by Elizabeth Silance Ballard:

There is a story many years ago of an elementary teacher. Her name was Mrs. Thompson. And as she stood in front of her 5th grade class on the very first day of school, she told the children a lie. Like most teachers, she looked at her students and said that she loved them all the same. But that was impossible, because there in the front row, slumped in his seat, was a little boy named Teddy.

Mrs. Thompson had watched Teddy the year before and noticed that he didn't play well with the other children, that his clothes were messy, and that he constantly needed a bath. And Teddy could be unpleasant. It got to the point where Mrs. Thompson would actually take delight in marking his papers with a broad red pen, making bold X's and then putting a big "F" at the top of his papers.

At the school where Mrs. Thompson taught, she was required to review each child's past records and she put Teddy's off until last. However, when she reviewed his file, she was in for a surprise.

Teddy's first grade teacher wrote, "Teddy is a bright child with a ready laugh. He does his work neatly and has good manners . . . he is a joy to be around." His second grade teacher wrote, "Teddy is an excellent student, well-liked by his classmates, but he is troubled because his mother has a terminal illness and life at home must be a struggle."

His third grade teacher wrote, "His mother's death has been hard on him. He tries to do his best but his father doesn't show much interest and his home life will soon affect him if some steps aren't taken."

Teddy's fourth grade teacher wrote, "Teddy is withdrawn and doesn't show much interest in school. He doesn't have many friends and sometimes sleeps in class."

By now, Mrs. Thompson realized the problem and she was ashamed of herself. She felt even worse when her students brought her Christmas presents, wrapped in beautiful ribbons and bright paper, except for Teddy's. His present was clumsily wrapped in the heavy, brown paper that he got from a grocery bag. Mrs. Thompson took pains to open it in the middle of the other presents. Some of the children started to laugh when she found a rhinestone bracelet with some of the stones missing and a bottle that was one quarter full of perfume. She stifled the children's laughter when she exclaimed how pretty the bracelet was, putting it on, and dabbing some of the perfume on her wrist.

Teddy stayed after school that day just long enough to say, "Mrs. Thompson, today you smelled just like my Mom used to." After the children left she cried for at least an hour.

On that very day, she quit teaching reading, and writing, and arithmetic. Instead, she began to teach children.

Mrs. Thompson paid particular attention to Teddy. As she worked with him, his mind seemed to come alive. The more she encouraged him, the faster he responded. By the end of the year, Teddy had become one of the smartest children in the class and, despite her lie that she would love all the children same, Teddy became one of her "teacher's pets."

A year later, she found a note under her door, from Teddy, telling her that she was still the best teacher he ever had in his whole life.

Six years went by before she got another note from Teddy. He then wrote that he had finished high school, second in his class, and she was still the best teacher he ever had in his whole life.

Four years after that, she got another letter, saying that while things had been tough at times, he'd stayed in school, had stuck with it, and would soon graduate from college with the highest of honors. He assured Mrs. Thompson that she was still the best and favorite teacher he ever had in his whole life.

Then four more years passed and yet another letter came. This time he explained that after he got his bachelor's degree, he decided to go a little further. The letter explained that she was still the best and favorite teacher he ever had. But now his name was a little longer. The letter was signed, Theodore F. Stollard, M.D.

The story doesn't end there. You see, there was yet another letter that spring. Teddy said he'd met this girl and was going to be married. He explained that his father had died a couple of years ago and he was wondering if Mrs. Thompson might agree to sit in the place at the wedding that was usually reserved for the mother of the groom.

Of course, Mrs. Thompson did. And guess what? She wore that bracelet, the one with several rhinestones missing. And she made sure she was wearing the perfume that Teddy remembered his mother wearing on their last Christmas together.

They hugged each other, and Teddy whispered in Mrs. Thompson's ear, "Thank you, Mrs. Thompson, for believing in me. Thank you so much for making me feel important and showing me that I could make a difference."

Mrs. Thompson, with tears in her eyes, whispered back. She said, "Teddy, you have it all wrong. You were the one who taught me that I could make a difference. I didn't know how to teach until I met you."[48]

Unfortunately, what we see is often what we get. And in Mrs. Thompson and Teddy's case, it could have proved disastrous. Like Mrs. Thompson, review your file. If you're not happy with what you see, change your perspective. You'll be one step closer to changing a life . . . or two.

---

48 Elizabeth Silance Ballard, "The Story of Teddy," *Educational Impact*, https://www.educationalimpact.com/resources/TeachChar/pdf/story_of_teddy.pdf.

CHAPTER 14

ATTITUDE OF GRATITUDE

S teve Harvey says, "Gratitude is one of the most overlooked key principles to your success."[49] And in a Forbes article, Luis. E. Romero continues:

Gratitude is the act of feeling and communicating apprecia-
tion for the people, circumstances and material possessions
in our lives. It allows us to cherish our present in ways that
make us feel in abundance rather than deprived.[50]

If your goal is to excel in life and soar to unimaginable heights, the way to get there is through gratitude. Showing gratitude has the ability to change your day. If you start your day with gratitude, then when the challenges come, they won't seem as severe because you'll be fortified with joy. It is said that success always leaves clues. One of the clues is gratitude. If you show me an individual who seems to continuously be elevated and advanced in life, I am most certain that the record will show that this is an individual filled with gratitude. This can be you.

49 Steve Harvey, "Gratitude Is One of the Most Overlooked and Key Principles to Your Success," *YouTube*, 17 Mar. 2022, https://www.youtube.com/watch?v=ZaQ1MY8xftE.
50 Luis E. Romero, "Gratitude: The Ultimate Spiritual Practice (a Thanksgiving Special)," *Forbes*, 22 Nov. 2017, https://www.forbes.com/sites/luisromero/2017/11/22/gratitude-the-ultimate-spiritual-practice-a-thanksgiving-special/?sh=6aed9acd2706.

I HAVE HEARD IT SAID THAT SUCCESS ALWAYS LEAVES CLUES, AND ONE OF THOSE CLUES IS GRATITUDE.

I believe that grace is a direct response to gratitude; the more grateful you are, the more grace steps in and mirrors the attitude that you have. Understand that what we appreciate in life appreciates—it grows and increases in value. What if the only things you could have to enjoy in life tomorrow were the things that you expressed gratitude for today? The people, the opportunities, the resources, the material things—if they were only equivalent to the things that you gave thanks for, I believe we would live differently. As you go through life, I am sure you have seen people that seemingly have everything, and they are blessed abundantly. However, they are miserable, unhappy, and ungrateful. On the other hand, I have seen people that have very little, are grateful for what they have, and are so very happy. (This is just a subjective thought, but maybe real happiness and serenity are not found in things but in gratitude.)

MAYBE REAL HAPPINESS AND SERENITY ARE NOT FOUND IN THINGS BUT IN GRATITUDE.

I believe that we all, ultimately, want to lead meaningful, fulfilled lives—lives that however and whenever we transition, people will say, "Wow! That person really made a great impact in life." Dr. Myles Monroe said, "The wealthiest place on earth is the cemetery. It holds the treasures that people never served to humanity."[51] How tragic that in it lie so many people that have taken all of their giftings and talents with them to the grave. I have determined that this will not be my fate. The most fulfilling thing in life for me is the thought of dying empty, having used all of the gifts and talents that the Creator placed inside of me for the betterment of His creation.

This, for me, is one of the greatest contributions we could ever make in life. Our daily attitude should be filled with love and gratitude that spills out of us and enriches other people's lives. Everything in life may not be perfect, but if the Creator allowed you to wake up this morning, you still have an opportunity to see the fulfillment of your life's dream. Start your day by counting your blessings and giving thanks for the many lessons that life has put you in a position to learn. Give thanks for having the strength to power through all of the lessons, all of the adversity, and all of the hard times. Give thanks because you know that God is going to see you through this.

Our hearts can be filled with gratitude because blessings flow in the space of gratitude. We should never be distraught over the things that did not work out in our lives because there's no such thing

51 Kingdom Grace, "Dr. Myles Munroe—the Wealthiest Place on Earth," *Kingdom Grace Media | Share4Christ - Christian Content Site*, 12 Feb. 2021, https://kingdomgracemedia.com/dr-myles-munroe-the-wealthiest-place-on-earth/.

as failure. Everything that we experience contains a lesson to be learned. And we can be grateful for those lessons because we are yet on the path to becoming the greatest expression of who we are.

When in a crisis, be grateful. When disappointed, be grateful. When your life seems to have been turned upside down, be grateful. I'm sure by now your thought is, *That's very easy to say when you are happy!* Think again. Is it really the happy people who are grateful, or is it the grateful people that are happy? The energy that you put out into the atmosphere is what will come back to you. When you show gratitude, it helps shield you from negativity. It makes you a happier person, and it helps you heal from stress and sleep better. It enhances your law of attraction.

WHEN IN A CRISIS, BE GRATEFUL. WHEN DISAPPOINTED, BE GRATEFUL. WHEN YOUR LIFE SEEMS TO HAVE BEEN TURNED UPSIDE DOWN, BE GRATEFUL.

When you give thanks and show gratitude, it improves your relationships because when people see that you have that aura of happiness, that glow is contagious, and it attracts the right people into your life. So begin to express gratitude in every situation, whether big or small, for all of the people in your inner space and for the people that you meet along the way.

A simple thing that could help you could be to get a journal and just start writing down all of the things that you are grateful for. You can start with just five or six things a day, and what you will find is that the more you focus and concentrate on what you are grateful for, the more you will see just how blessed you really are. If you sincerely want to be happy, take a moment and begin to count all of the beautiful things that you have. I understand that my life is a gift that has been given to me by the Creator and that I must show continued appreciation and gratitude for this gift. My appreciation draws other things to me that money can't buy: peace, happiness, and contentment.

The time I've spent writing *Mindset–Reset* has been a period of reflection in this season of my life. I have come to know the true God of the heavens and earth in a way that I have never known Him. I celebrated thirty-five years of life, love, and commitment to the girl of my dreams. I reflected on watching our one seed, our son, Darius, grow, develop, and mature into the man that he is, with a wife and a daughter. I considered my godchildren and my siblings, and I have been thinking about the place that I am in my life right now.

The ministry that I serve is extremely blessed, and I was sharing with someone the other day that the people that serve in ministry with me have hearts of gold. They love God, and they so willingly serve Him by giving of their gifts and talents in ministry for His kingdom. The atmosphere is filled with love, peace, and brotherhood. People that visit all say that they feel so much love upon entering our house, and in a world that is so filled with hurt, pain, and disappointment, it is such an honor to be in a house that's filled with love for all people. For this, we are grateful.

Gratitude is the best medicine there is. It heals your mind, body, and spirit, and it ultimately attracts more things for you to be grateful for, so I implore you to wake up each and every day and give thanks. Be grateful for the things that you have in your life. If you can do that, you can live your best life right now!

Thanksgiving or gratitude is one of the key producers of the supernatural. In its essence, gratitude is a practical orientation to a lifestyle of genuine and continued appreciation for the acts of God in one's life. If there were ever a time that we needed the supernatural power of God to show up in our lives, it's now! When this principle is demonstrated in your life, I believe that you will see and begin to walk in the supernatural like never before. We must adopt a practical orientation to a lifestyle of giving continuous gratitude to God for the things He has done!

IN ITS ESSENCE, GRATITUDE IS A PRACTICAL ORIENTATION TO A LIFESTYLE OF GENUINE AND CONTINUED APPRECIATION FOR THE ACTS OF GOD IN ONE'S LIFE.

The scripture, "In everything give thanks; for this is the will of God in Christ Jesus for you," (1 Thessalonians 5:18, NKJV) is saying that no matter what situation you are in, whether it's something good or something that could be considered bad, you can continually appreciate God for His wonderful acts. And in all of life's circumstances, you need to be able to pull from your life's file and remember what God has done in the past. Bring that feeling of euphoria into your present, and the supernatural will begin to manifest for you. God is waiting for your gratitude to perfect His plan and purpose for your life

Take a minute and just remember what God has done because thanksgiving is the doorway to the supernatural power of God being revealed in your life! Gratitude gets the attention of heaven. If you fail to appreciate God, your life will depreciate with time.

CHAPTER 15

CLOSING THOUGHTS

Reprogramming is a type of reset. Are we running our lives with the conscious mind, or are subconscious programs running our lives for us? A recent study at Auburn University suggests that only during 5 percent of the day are we operating according to our conscious minds' creative wishes and desires while 95 percent of the day our lives are coming straight out of the programs in our subconscious.52 It's a problem if 95 percent of the day we're operating from these programs, and the vast majority of them, in the words of Dr. Bruce Liptman, are "disempowering and self-sabotaging downloads."53 Therefore, we must constantly apply the principles we have discussed in Mindset–Reset that will enable us to rewrite the downloads we have received over the years.

Principle #1—Working on your inner healing is a lifelong process. When you first start to work on your inner healing, you will experience feelings of depression and pain. It may frustrate you, but if you keep pressing through and working on it, it will become

---

52 Marianne Szegedy-Maszak, "Your Unconscious Is Making Your Everyday Decisions," *Mysteries of the Mind*, http://webhome.auburn.edu/~mitrege/ENGL2210/USNWR-mind.html#:~:text=According%20to%20 cognitive%20neuroscientists%2C%20we,goes%20beyond%20our%20conscious%20awareness.
53 Bruce Lipton, PhD, "Reprogram Your Subconscious Mind with These 3 Powerful Steps," *Fearless Soul*, 8 July 2019, https://iamfearlesssoul.com/reprogram-your-subconscious-mind-with-these-3-powerful-steps-bruce-lipton/.

rewarding. Dr. John Kehoe studied the subconscious mind for over thirty-nine years. He believes that people can reprogram their subconscious mind, and there are clear steps a person can take to do it, but it takes some effort.[54] Perhaps people are too lazy to do the work that they need to do to reprogram the subconscious mind.

Principle #2—Devoting yourself to the right response is possible through God's strength. Deep within us, there is a force that has the ability to guide us into a fruitful and successful life. The inner conflict of the struggle between the waking mind and the sleeping mind is ever true and prevalent; therefore, we must remain committed to the task of mastering our thought processes in this ever-raging war. Despite the ups and downs of life, there is one constant, and it is the cumulation of the power, the grace, and the love of God. It will forever be with us. It is a great consolation to know that the everlasting God, the Creator of the heavens and the earth, is rooting for me, and He's rooting for you. Partner with Him. Take charge of *your* world, and create the next great invention that will change the course of *the* world forever.

Working on inner healing and devoting yourself to the right response can seem tricky at first, but they are really quite simple. At the outset, if you commit to it, you will change your thoughts which will change your emotions which will ultimately change your world. We have a choice to make: Will we master our thoughts and change the world? Or will we allow our thoughts to master us and remain the same?

---

54 John Kehoe, "Advices from Mind Power Pioneer on Making Our Each Day the Way We Want It to Be," *YouTube*, 11 June 2020, https://www.youtube.com/watch?v=fKDmD7K37wY.

WE HAVE A CHOICE TO MAKE: WILL WE MASTER OUR THOUGHTS AND CHANGE THE WORLD? OR WILL WE ALLOW OUR THOUGHTS TO MASTER US AND REMAIN THE SAME?

I would like to leave you with an affirmation to repeat out loud three times a day:

> *"The creative intelligence of my subconscious mind (God) knows what is best for me in every situation and circumstance. His intention is always to prosper me and bring me to His expected end. At all times, He reveals to me the right answer for every situation I face."*

Let us follow the apostle Paul's admonition in Colossians 3:9-10 (ESV) and "put off the old self with its practices and . . . put on the new self, which is being renewed in knowledge after the image of its creator."

CONTACT INFORMATION

Facebook group:

http://www.facebook.com/groups/iminspired.me/

Website: http://iminspired.me/

Email: Breakingbarrierscoach@gmail.com

CPSIA information can be obtained
at www.ICGtesting.com
Printed in the USA
BVHW030509190922
647081BV00007B/18